Bull Terrier, Bull Terrier Training AAA AKC: Think Like a Dog, but Don't Eat Your Poop! | Bull Terrier Breed Expert Training | Here's EXACTLY How to Train Your Bull Terrier

By Paul Allen Pearce

The Bull Terrier

As a child growing up in America and living in a household that allowed me to watch "Baa Baa Black Sheep" I was exposed to heavy doses of this peculiar looking dog breed. I had never seen one until I tuned into the WWII highflying dysfunctional show of fighter pilots always breaking the rules and fighting. Due to this, I associate this dog with being a tough, rebellious breed, and I am still entertained by its peculiar facial and muzzle appearance. "It's so ugly that it's cute" is a saying that comes to mind.

What the heck is the background story to this large, stout, quirky dog breed? At the time during the early 1800's crosses of Bulldog's and terriers were common. The sporting crowd used many of these dogs for fighting and wagering. Around the early 1860's, James Hinks of Birmingham, England decided he would make his own cross and it would be the popular color of the time, all white. This pure white color became the hallmark of the early Bull Terriers. Hink went to work to breed a more refined and consistent cross breed dog. He used his own Bulldog, *Madman*, the White English Terrier, and possibly the Dalmatian. His quest was to make a gentleman's dog, and it later gained the name White Cavalier. The product was a pure white, shorthaired, muscular dog. He had a success on his hands and soon people were collecting their own Cavalier's for show pets and companions.

By 1897, their popularity had spread across the Atlantic Ocean and had risen to such heights that the Bull Terrier Club of America had already been established. After a while, the Bull Terrier was crossed with colored Staffordshire Bull Terrier's and color patches surfaced, and later this became acceptable in the standard by making in 1936 an additional classification for colored Bull Terriers.

This sometimes intimidating, bizarre, or frightening looking dog is not as it seems, this dog is a children loving, family loving, affectionate, sweetheart of a dog. Yep, they love children, but they are powerful and should be properly socialized and chaperoned around children, cats, and other family dogs. They have a strong prey drive that puts into danger other animals including your cat. Their over-protective nature can also rise up and show itself. Proper and thorough socialization is a necessity for this breed to keep their behavioral issues to themselves. Although he may befriend your household cat this does not mean the neighbor's cat is safe around your new best friend.

Feisty, and clownish; they make an entertaining and loyal companion that are readily available for play. Bullies rarely bark so if you hear them bark, be sure to look and see the cause. This breed needs to be in the company of others and needs this stimulus to remain mentally healthy. Their coat requires almost no grooming, just brush a couple of times a week, and do all the other basic grooming dog needs. You can get away with only bathing every three months and you will enjoy that this breed has a low doggy odor.

A few health concerns to be aware are slipped patella (dislocation of the kneecaps), heart defects, kidney failure, eye disorders, and skin and flea allergies. They are prone to suffer from a zinc deficiency, which can cause death. If not properly exercised they easily gain weight, so be sure to not over-feed. All white Bullies are prone to deafness and should be tested. They chill easily, so keep your Bull Terrier indoors and warm. They are not meant to sleep outdoors.

When you have a dog with a strong prey drive and they are engaged in the chase, you tend to get a breed that enjoys pulling their masters down the street, across the lawn, through the park, across the stream, and even into oncoming traffic. Add to that formula, size, weight, and strength and you understand why you are motivated to have an obedient Bull Terrier as your companion. You can't train the prey drive out of a dog, but you can train your dog to listen and obey your commands, and with fingers crossed, most of the time your Bully will listen and obey.

When your Bully is a puppy be sure that he learns "no", "leave it", and "stay", before you begin walking your seventy-pound plus full grown dog around the neighborhood. Please read the information on *socialization* inside this guide and others, and follow the steps from the time you get your new shiny puppy home. Establish yourself in the *alpha* position as the provider of all good things, caretaker, schedule maker, consistent, calm, fun, leader, and trainer of Bullies. Your goal is to have a thoroughly socialized dog that is obedient and understands the rules of behavior in all situations that your Bully will encounter. There must be no challenging or questioning that you are the leader, and your rules must be followed. Bullies will test your authority, and definitely your patience.

This dog has the energy to run around all day, so be sure to give them long daily walks where you practice the heel command. Give them time to play, and only let them off leash to roam when they are in a safe fenced in area.

 As we know, many Terriers are diggers, so just in case you find yourself with a digging Bully, I am including this. Some dogs are going to dig no matter what you do, it is bred into them, and they have the urge to keep on digging. Remember that when you have a digger for a dog that they tend to be escape artists, so you need to bury your perimeter fencing deep to keep them inside the yard.

A solution is to dig a pit specifically for him or her to dig to their little heart's content. Pick out the location, turn over the soil a bit to loosen it up, mix in some sand to keep it loose and improve drainage, then surround it with stones or bricks to make it obvious for the dog by sight.

To begin training bury bones, chews, or a favorite toy, and coax your dog on over to the pit to dig up some treasures. Keep a watchful eye on your dog each time you bring him out, and do not leave him unsupervised. Quickly halt any digging outside the pit. When he digs in the designated pit, be sure to reward him with treats and praise. If he digs elsewhere, direct him back to the pit, keep it full, and if necessary keep burying things he wants to dig up.

One last thing that can assist is to place your dogs own *doodie* into the holes. When your dog returns he will not enjoy the surprise. ~ *Enjoy your Bull Terrier dog!*

Introduction

Who is "man's best friend?" My wife says it's the couch, a pizza and ESPN, but that is because she grew up with four brothers. However, we all know man's best friend is his dog. I love my dog. I love dogs. They provide comfort, support, undying love, and someone to bounce all those brilliant ideas off that are going to make you a millionaire someday. I cannot imagine life without my dog.

When I picked Axel up and brought him home, he was a puppy. I was advised to train him well and not to make him a guard or an attack dog. Actually, training your dog makes him happier, healthier, and much more stable. Who knew?

With that in mind, I embarked on the journey of training this little puppy. Diving in head first, I bought books, acquired videos, and even talked with professional trainers about the matter. Over time, I gleaned a lot of helpful information. I learned about commonly encountered behavioral problems, and some not so common as well. I absorbed facts about proper diet, exercise, and training techniques. Because of my interest and commitment to his best interest, my dog is well behaved, happy, social, and understands a point spread better than any other dog traveling in the car pool lane.

While I was going through the process of learning how to train my puppy, I noticed one thing; *trainers are really, really,* serious about their craft, but will my lack of seriousness result in a poorly trained dog? The informality of my approach has resulted in a fabulous companion that clumsily bumps around the house, and chews on this and that in pure puppy form. Whether he's curled up snoozing or striking an adorable pose, the real joy comes simply from his mere presence, and of these joys, the laughter that he incites is at the very top of the list.

Keeping laughter and light heartedness in mind as a dog owner in training, is of the utmost importance because sometimes training can be very difficult on you and your pal. Sometimes your dog will push your patience to the limits. Remember to try and never let your dog know that you are at your limits. You are given the awesome responsibility at the time of acquisition, to be the pack leader and ultimately your dog's sensei.

I kept that in mind when I sat down to put this rewards based training book together. What I hope you will find inside here is a complete, concise training guide, the information of which is culled from trainers, training manuals and years of experience with a wonderful dog. Though this guide approaches training as a serious endeavor, your dog will teach you that it will not always be serious, and nor should you. I have attempted to infuse his playful spirit throughout this instructional. I hope that those light moments within this reading will help you get through the tougher times, like the chewing of your cell phone, the pooping on your socks and those mysterious expenses charged to your credit card. "Could it be that only Axel is able to run a credit card via telephone?"

A dog can be a loyal and longtime friend, worthy of your commitment and care. Your dog can give your life so much richness, and in return, asks very little. If you train him well, he or she will be happier, and as science has proven, so will you. If you keep a sense of humor alive during training, the outcomes will be the best for both of you. I hope you find this guide informative, easy to follow and fun.   Enjoy.

Table of Contents

Getting Social with Your Bull Terrier

Socializing your puppy, especially before the age of six months, is a very important step in preventing future behavioral problems. Socializing can and should continue throughout the life of your dog. Socializing in a gentle and kind manner prevents aggressive, fearful, and potential behaviors with possible litigious outcomes. A lack of socializing may lead to fear, aggression, barking, shyness, or hyperactivity, and the risk of wearing Goth make up and the smoking of clove cigarettes. The earlier you start socializing, the better. However, all puppies and dogs can gradually be brought into new and initially frightening situations, eventually learning to enjoy them. Canines can adapt to various and sometimes extreme situations, they just need your calm, guiding hand.

Expect that the socializing of your dog will be a lifelong endeavor. If your puppy does not engage with other dogs for months or years at a time, you can expect his behavior to be different when he encounters them again. I mean, how would you feel if your sixth grade math teacher who you haven't seen in 22 years, just walked up and sniffed you?

Here are some methods you can use when exposing your dog to something new, or something he has previously been distrustful contacting:

- Remain calm, upbeat and if he has a leash on, keep it loose.

- Gradually expose him to the new stimulus and if he is wary or fearful never use force. Let him retreat if he needs to.

- Reward him using treats; give him a good scratch or an energetic run for being calm and exploring new situations.

Try on a regular basis to expose your dog to the things that you would like him to be capable to cope. His gained familiarity will allow him to calmly deal with such situations in the future. Be careful of the same old-same old. Though dogs love routine, periodically expose your dog to new things. This allows you to assess his need for further socialization. You certainly wouldn't want to go on vacation to the same place every single year, so why would he.

Examples of situations that benefit the social temperament of your Bully:

- Meeting new kinds of people, including but not limited to, children, crowds, people wearing hats, disabled folks, and people in local services such as postal carriers, fire and police officers, and more. "Introducing your puppy to a circus clown is saved for another chapter."

- Meeting new dogs is encouraged. Because of canine diseases, be aware that you should wait at least 4 months before introducing your puppy to dog parks or places where there are groups of adult dogs. You can begin puppy socialization classes at around 7 weeks, just be sure your puppy has a round of vaccines at least a week prior. Slowly expose your dog to other pets, such as cats, horses, birds, llamas, pigs, gerbils, and monitor lizards.

- His crate is not a jail. Be sure and take the time to teach your puppy to enjoy the comfort and privacy of his own crate. We will be going over instructions on this in the section, Housetraining.

"Well! That's Not Good Behavior!"

How to deal with a problem behavior before it becomes a habit

Everyone likes his or her own space to feel comfy, familiar, and safe. Your dog is no different. A proper living space is a key factor to avoiding all kinds of potential problems. Think of all the things your puppy will encounter in his life with humans. Things like baths, walks, radio, T.V., neighbors, visitors, the vacuum, and so forth that are not necessarily familiar or common in nature, and can be frightening to your dog. It is essential to use treats, toys, and praise to assist you and your dog while in the midst of training and socializing.

Dogs are social creatures and it is essential to communicate with them. Communication is always the key to behavior reinforcement. If his good, calm behavior is frequently rewarded and you have control over his favorite things, this acts as a pathway to solving problems that may arise down the road.

Keep your dog's world happy. Make sure he is getting a proper amount of exercise and that he is being challenged mentally. Make sure he is getting enough time in the company of other dogs and other people. Keep a close eye on his diet, offering him good, healthy, dog-appropriate foods. A small treat every now and then is perfectly in order. Avoid excessive helpings during treating.

It is important that you be a strong leader. Dogs are pack animals and your dog needs to know that you are the alpha. Do not let situations fall into that questionable "who's the boss?" scenario. Your puppy will feel confident and strong if he works for his rewards and knows that he or she has a strong, confident leader to follow. Let him show you good behavior before you pile on the goodies, or a new roof on his doghouse. With a little work on his part, he will appreciate it more.

Getting by the challenges

Your dog's first step towards overcoming the challenges in life is in understanding what motivates his own behavior. Some behaviors your dog will exhibit are instinctual. Barking, chewing, jumping, digging, chasing, and leash pulling are things that all dogs do because it is in their genetic make-up. These natural behaviors differ from the ones we have inadvertently trained into the domestic canine. Behaviors such as barking for attention or nudging our hands asking to be petted are actually accidently reinforced by us humans and not innate.

What motivates your dog to do what he does or does not do? You may wonder why he does not come when you call him while he is playing with other dogs. Simply, this may be because coming to you is far less exciting than scrapping with the same species. When calling your dog you can change this behavior simply by offering him a highly coveted treat and afterward allow him to continue playing for a while. Start this training aspect slowly, and in short distances from where he is playing.

Here are some helpful tips to use when trying to help your Bull Terrier through challenging behavior.

- Think about the quality of his diet and health. Is your dog getting enough playtime, mental and physical exercise, and sleep? Is this a medical problem? Do not ignore the range of possibilities that could be eliciting his challenging behavior.

- Are you accidentally rewarding bad behavior? Remember that your dog may see any response from you as a reward. You can ignore the misbehavior if you are patient enough, or you can give your puppy the equivalent of a human "time out" for a few minutes. Make sure the time out environment is in a calm, quiet and safe, but very dull place, similar to my grandma's condo in Florida.

- Be sure and practice replacement behavior. Reward him with something that is much more appealing than the perceived reward that he is getting when he is misacting. It is important to reward his good behavior before he misacts. If done consistently and correctly, this will reinforce good behaviors, and reduce poor behaviors. For example, if your dog jumps up to get love, teach him to sit instead by only giving him love after he sits and never if he jumps up onto you. If you command, "sit" and he complies and you pat him on the head or speak nicely to him, or both, your dog will associate the sitting compliance with nice things. If he jumps and you turn away and never acknowledge him he will understand that is not associated with nice things. In this scenario, you want to catch him before he leaps and then immediately say, "sit"

While practicing the replacement behavior, be sure you reward the right response and ignore the mistakes. Remember, any response to the wrong action could be mistaken as a reward by your dog, so try to remain neutral in a state of ignoring. Be sure to offer your dog a greater reward for the correct action than the joy he is getting from doing the wrong action. You will have to think up counter actions for each wrong action you are replacing.

- Your dog's bad behavior may be caused by something that causes him fear. If you decipher this as the problem try to change his mind about what he perceives frightening. Pair the scary thing with something he loves. Say your dog has a problem with the local skateboarder. Pair the skateboarder's visit with a super treat and lots of attention. He will soon look forward to the daily arrival of the skateboarder.

- Always, remain patient with your dog and do not force changes. Work gradually and slowly. Forcing behavioral changes on your dog may lead making the behaviors worse.

~ Paws On – Paws Off ~

Rewards not Punishment

It is always better to reward your Bully instead of punishing him. Here are a few reasons why:

- If you punish your dog, it can make him distrust, fear, and avoid you. If you rub your dog's nose in it, he may avoid going to the bathroom in front of you. This is going to make his public life difficult.

- Electric fences will make him avoid the yard and choke collars can cause injuries to his throat as well as cause back and neck misalignment.

- Physical punishment has the tendency to escalate in severity. If you get your dog's attention by a light tap on the nose, he will soon get used to that and ignore it. Soon the contact will become more and more violent. As we know, violence is *not* the answer.

- Punishing your dog may have some bad side effects. For example, if you are using a pinch collar, it may tighten when he encounters other dogs. Dogs are very smart, but they aren't always logical. When your dog encounters another dog, the pinching of the collar may lead him to think the other dog is the reason for the pinch. Pinch collars have been linked to the reinforcement of aggressive behaviors between dogs.

- You may inadvertently develop and adversarial relationship with your dog if you punish him instead of working through a reward system. If you only look for the mistakes with your dog, this is all you will begin to see. In your mind, you will see a problem dog. In your dog's mind, he will see anger and distrust.

- You ultimately want to change your dog's incorrect actions into acceptable actions. By punishing your dog, he will learn only to *avoid* punishment. He is not learning to change the behavior you want changed, instead he learns to be sneaky or to do the very minimum to avoid being punished. Your dog can become withdrawn and seemingly inactive. Permanent psychological damage can be done if a dog lives in fear of punishment.

- If you punish rather than reward neither you nor your dog will be having a very good time. It will be a constant, sometimes painful struggle. If you have children, they will not be able to participate in a punishment based training process because it is too difficult, and truly no fun.

- Simply put, if you train your dog using rewards, you and your dog will have a much better time. Rely on rewards to change his behavior by using treats, toys, playing, petting, affection, or anything else you know your dog likes. If your dog is doing something that you do not like, replace the habit with another by teaching him to do something different, and then reward him for doing the replacement action, and then you can all enjoy the outcome.

~ *Paws On – Paws Off* ~

Training: Things that Work

Knowing what you want to train your dog to do is as important as training your dog. You can begin training almost immediately, at around six weeks of age. A puppy is a blank slate and does not know any rules, therefore it is a wise idea to make a list and have an understanding of what you would like your puppy to do. As he grows, the same principle applies and you may adjust training from the basics to more specialized behaviors, such as making your dog a good travel, hiking, agility, hunting, or simply a companion dog. Know what conditions and circumstances you plan to expose your dog or puppy to outside of the household and strategize to be prepared for those encounters by slowly introducing him to those situations.

Establish yourself as the pack leader from the time you first bring your new dog or puppy home. Being the *alpha* assists in the training process, and your dogs relationship with you and your family. Life is much easier for your dog if you are in charge, leading, and providing for his needs. Leading as the alpha assists in the act of working together with your dog towards the goal of understanding the rules of conduct and obedience. Your dog will be at ease when the rules are understood. Training should be an enjoyable bonding time between you and your dog. Remember that there is no set time limit defining when your dog should learn, understand, and then obey commands. Use short training sessions and be aware that if either of you are tired, it is recommended that you stop and try again later. If something does not seem quite right with your dog, in any way, have him checked out by a veterinarian.

Timing is crucial when rewarding for good behaviors and making corrections for bad.

Patience and Consistency are your allies in the training game. An easy way to avoid the onset of many different behavioral problems is to give your dogs or puppies ample daily exercise to keep them fit and healthy, and destructive behavioral problems at bay. Always provide consistent structure, firm authority, rule enforcement, and importantly, love and affection. By maintaining these things, you will help to create a loyal companion and friend. Reward good behaviors, not for simply being cute, sweet, loveable, and huggable. If you wish to reward your dog, always reward after you issue a command and your dog obeys appropriately. Keep your training sessions short, with variety and an abundance of different treats and rewards. The most important thing to remember is to remain relaxed, keep it fun, and enjoy this time of bonding and training of your dog or puppy.

All dogs have their own personalities and therefore respond to training differently. No matter the breed that usually comes with its own characteristics, you need to account for individual personality and adjust accordingly.

We all love treats, and so does your dog. Giving your dog a treat is the best way to reinforce good behavior, to help change his behavior or just to make him do that insanely funny dance- like-thing he does. Make the treats small enough for him to get a taste, but not a meal, kernel sized. Remember, you do not want him filling up on treats as it might spoil his dinner and interfere with his attention span.

- Keep a container of treats handy with you at all times. You do not want to miss a chance to reward a good behavior or reinforce a changed behavior. Always carry treats when you go on a walk. Remember what treats your dog likes most and save those for super special times. In addition, what you consider a treat and what your dog considers a treat are two vastly different worlds. A single malt scotch or chicken wings might be a treat in your mind, but dried liver bits or beef jerky in your dogs.

- Ask for something before you give the treat. Tell your dog to sit, stay, or lie down, print two copies of your resume, anything, before you reward him with treats, petting, or play. By asking for good behavior, before you give him a reward you demonstrate you are in charge, in an easy fun manner. There is a common misconception that dogs are selfless and wanting to behave only to please out of respect for you. This is horse pucky. This line of thinking is incorrect and detrimental to your success with the training. You have to make sure that your dog knows exactly why he should be listening to you. You are the alpha, the keeper of the treats, the provider of the scratching and the purveyor of toys. Keep this balance of power and the results will be your reward.

- Be positive. Think about what you want your dog to do instead of what you don't want him to do. Do not send mixed messages. Simply, ignore the bad behavior and reward when your dog when he does what you want to be done. Teach your dog some simple commands to communicate what you want, such as, "drop it," or "leave it".

- Keep the training sessions short at 15 minutes maximum per session. You will be continuously training your companion, but use the formal training sessions to focus on one objective. Any session longer than 15 minutes will be hard for your dog to stay focused. During training, this is the attention span of most canines.

- Run, run, run! It goes without saying, that your dog will be much happier if you run him every day. Run your dog until his tongue is hanging out. If he is still full of energy, run him again and he will love you for this. A little exercise before a training session to release some of your dog's energy can increase his ability to focus during the session.

- Kids are great, are they not? However, the notion that kids and dogs are as natural a pairing as chocolate and peanut butter is simply just not true. Kids are often bitten by dogs because they unintentionally do things that frighten dogs. Sometime a child's behavior appears like prey to a dog. Never leave a dog and a child together unsupervised, even if the dog is 'good' with children. Teach children not to approach a dog that is unfamiliar to them. The way a child behaves with the familiar family dog, may not be appropriate with another dog they meet for the first time.

- It is very important that you make sure your dog is comfortable in all sorts of situations. All dogs, even your sweet tempered Bully, have the potential to bite. Making sure, he is comfortable in various situations and teaching your dog to be gentle with his mouth will reduce the risk of unwanted bites.

~ Paws On – Paws Off ~

Clicker Training Your Bully

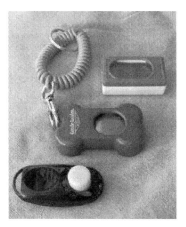

What the heck is that clicking noise? Well, it's a clicker, thus the name. If you are a product of a Catholic school, you might be very familiar with this device. You probably have nightmares of large, penguin like women clicking their way through your young life. Yes, it was annoying and at times, terrifying, however, when it comes to training your dog, it will be helpful and fun.

A clicker is a small device that makes a sound that is easily distinguished and not common as a sound in nature, or one that humans normally produce. This unique sound keeps the dog that is being trained from becoming confused by accidently hearing a word used in conversation or another environmental noise. You click when your dog does the correct action then immediately follow the click with a treat or reward

The clicker is used to inform your dog that he did the right thing and that a treat is coming. When your dog does the right thing after you command, like drop your Chanel purse that is dangling from his mouth, you click and reward him with a nice treat. Using the clicker system allows you to set your puppy up to succeed while you ignore or make efforts to prevent bad behavior. It is a very positive, humane system and punishment is *not* part of the process.

Here are some questions often asked about the clicker training:

- "Do you need to have the clicker on your person at all times?" *No.* The clicker is a teaching device. Once your dog understands what you want him to do, you can then utilize a verbal or hand cue.

- "With all these treats, isn't my dog going to get fat?" *No.* If you figure treats into your dog's daily intake and subtract from meals accordingly, your dog will be fine. The treats should be small, perhaps just a taste. Use food from his regular meals when you are training indoors, but when outdoors, use fresh treats like meat or cheese. There are many distractions outside and a tasty fresh treat will help keep your puppy's attention.

- "Can rewards be other things besides treats?" *Sure.* Actually, you should mix it up. Use the clicker and a treat when you first start teaching. When your puppy has learned the behavior you want, and then switch to other rewards, such as, petting, play, or lottery tickets. Remember always to ask for the wanted target behavior, such as, *sit, stay,* or come before you reward your dog. These verbal reinforcements can augment the clicker training and reward giving.

-"What do I do if my dog disobeys a command?" *Simple,* if your dog disobeys you, it is because he has not been properly trained. Sorry, but you have to take the responsibility for that. He, after all, is just a dog. You, on the other hand, have the driver's license. You wield the power. If he is disobeying, he has had poor training or the treats are not tasty enough. Try simplifying the task and attempt to make the reward equal to, or better than what is distracting him.

HELPFUL HINT

- *Conceal the treat! Do NOT* show your dog the treat before pressing the clicker, and make the clicking sound. If you do this, he will be responding to the treat and not the click and this will *undermine* your training strategy.

~ *Paws On – Paws Off* ~

Let's Talk Treats

You are training your puppy and he is doing well, *of course*, because he is the best dog in the world! *Oh yes he is.* Because of this fact, you want to make sure that you're giving him the right kind of treats. Treats are easy. As long as you stay away from the things that aren't good for dogs, such as; avocado, onions, garlic, coffee, tea, caffeinated drinks, grapes, raisins, macadamia nuts, peaches, plums, pits, seeds, persimmons, chocolate, whiskey & soda, Guinness Stout, just to name a few.

You can make treats from many different foods. First, treats should be small, kernel sized, and easy to grab from a pocket or concealable container. When you are outdoors and there are many distractions, treats should be of a higher quality and coveted by your pooch, we call it a higher value treat because it is worthy of your dog breaking away from the activity he is engaged Perhaps cubes of cheese, dried meat, special kibble or the neighbor cat (just joking all you cat lovers). Make sure you mix it up and keep a variety of snacks available when you are out and about. Nothing is worse during treat training than your dog or puppy turning his nose up at a treat because he has grown bored of it.

Here are some treat ideas:

- Cubed meats that preferably are not highly processed or salted.

- Shredded cheese, string cheese or cubed cheese. Dogs love cheese!

- Cream cheese, peanut butter, or easy cheese. Give your dog a small dollop to lick for every proper behavior.

- No sugar, whole grain cereals are good. Cheerios are good choice. No need for milk, bowl, or spoon. You can just give him the goods, as is.

- Kibble (dry foods). Put some in a paper bag and boost the aroma factor by tossing in some bacon or another meat product. Dogs are all about those yummy smell sensations.

- Beef Jerky. Preferably with no pepper or heavy seasoning.

- Carrot, apple pieces, and some dogs even enjoy melons.

- Baby food meat products. You know, those strange little suspect pink sausage things.

- Commercial dog treats. Be careful, there as there are tons of them on the market. Look for those that do not have preservatives, by products, or artificial colors.

- Ice cube. Not the rap star but the frozen water treats. Your dog will love crunching these up

Avoid feeding your hairy friend from the dining table; because you do not want to teach him to beg when people are sitting down to eat. Give treats far from the dinner table or a good distance from where people gather to eat.

~ *Paws On* — *Paws Off* ~

Part II: Begin School – Name Recognition

Now we are going to teach your puppy some specific things. Let us start with a base exercise of getting your puppy to respond to his or her *name*. I assume that you have named your puppy and now you want him or her to learn its name. This can be easy and fun.

- Get a nice variety of treats and put them in your pockets, treat pouch, or on a tabletop out of sight and reach. When your dog looks at you, say his name, then, give him a treat. *Simple.*

- Responding to his name is the most important behavior and it is going to form the base of all the other things you will be teaching him later on. Therefore, you will want to spend the time and give this a considerable amount of attention. Repeat the exercise all around the house while he is on the leash, outside in the yard or in the park. Make sure you practice this while there are distractions, such as when there are guests present, when his favorite toys are visible, when there is food around, and when he is among other dogs. Call your dog's name and give him a treat while maintaining good eye contact is optimal. This will avoid trouble later on down the line. For example, if your puppy gets into something that he should not, such as a scrap with another dog, chasing a cat, squirrel, or a time-share pyramid scheme, you can call your dog's name and he will come for the treat. After time and practice, he will eventually come only because you command it.

- It may sound odd, but also try to doing this when you are in different positions such as sitting, standing, or lying down. Mix it up so that he gets used to hearing his name in a variety of situations. No matter the situation, this command must be obeyed. Before moving forward be certain your puppy knows and responds to his name being called. Continue this into adulthood to be certain you are able to grab your dog's attention in any circumstance.

~ *Paws On – Paws Off* ~

"Come" An Important Command

After your puppy recognizes and begins responding to his name being called, then the "come!" command is the one that you want to teach next. *Why?* Because this one could save his life, save your sanity, and save you running through the neighborhood in the middle of the night wearing little more than a robe and slippers.

If by chance he is checking out the olfactory magic of the trash bin, the best way to redirect your dog is to yell, *"come!"* followed by an immediate reward when he does. Petting or play is an appropriate reinforcement incentive for this type of situation.

Here's what to do-

- Think *treats.* Find a quiet, low distraction place so both of you can focus. Place a treat on the floor and walk to the other side of the room. Next, hold out a hand with a new treat in it. Next, say your dog's name to get his attention, followed by the command "come". Use a pleasant, happy tone when you do this. As he starts to come to you, praise him all the way to the treat. Do this about a dozen times and then take a break. For the next session, you can request the assistance of a family member and have them stand at a distance (5-6 paces) opposite you, next take turns calling your dog back and forth between you. Do this a dozen times. The object is to reinforce to your dog the idea that coming to his name is not only for you, but is beneficial to him as well.

- Next, as before, put a treat on the ground, move across the room, and then call his name to get his attention. This time, hold out an empty hand and give the command. This will mess with him a little, but that is okay. As soon as he starts to come to you, give him praise. When he gets to you, give him a treat from your pocket or pouch. Do this about a dozen times and then take a break.

- Keep practicing this with an empty hand, and this training will eventually become a hand signal. You then want to take this another step by fading out the hand signal and just using a verbal cue. Make sure your dog is coming on command with each cue.

Let's get complex

- Try practicing this exercise out of your dog's sight. Practice outside in increasingly more distracting situations. Start with a treat in hand, then fade the exercise to just the hand and finally using only the verbal command.

The Decoy Exercise, "Fetchus Interrupts" and Hide & Seek

- *The Decoy*. One person calls the dog; we will call this person the *handler*. One person tries to distract the dog with food, and toys; we will call this person the *teaser*. When the dog goes toward the teaser, they should turn away from the dog. When the dog goes toward the handler, he should be rewarded by both the handler and the teaser.

- *Interrupting the Fetch or "Fetchus Interruptus."* Get a good-sized handful of his dry food. Then, toss a ball or a piece of food. As your dog is in the process of chasing it, call him by name. If he comes *after* he gets the ball/food, give him a little reward of one piece of treat. If he comes *before* he gets the ball/food, give him a handful (7-10) of treats. After you've thrown the ball/food a few times, it's time to change it up. Now, fake throwing something and call him. If he goes looking for the ball/food before he comes to you, give a small treat. If he comes immediately, give the huge treat. "Another application for this training can be effective with your teenagers."

- *Hide & Seek.* While you are outside and your dog is distracted and doesn't seem to know you exist, *hide*. When your dog comes looking for you, and finds you, reward him with lots of love and treats. Make it seem like an extremely big deal that he found you, by adding a little drama.

HELPFUL HINTS

- Never, call your Bully for something he might find unpleasant. If you are leaving the park, call him, put on the leash and play a little more. This will pacify and distract.

- Make sure that his coming to you is always the best thing ever. Always treat, praise, and when appropriate, play with a ball or toy as an additional reinforcement.

- You are calling, and your puppy is not responding. What do you do now? Try running backwards away from him, crouch, and clap, and then show him a toy or food. When he comes, still reward him even though he stressed you out. Running towards your do signals to play catch *me*, so avoid doing this.

- If your dog has been off the lead for a while, remember to give him a treat when he checks in with you

- You should practice "come!" five to ten times daily, forever. It is one of those potentially life-saving commands and helps with all daily activities and interactions. The goal is that your dog will come running whether you are in or out of sight and from any audible distance.

~ *Paws On – Paws Off* ~

"Drop it" A Must Learn

Teaching your Bully to *drop it* is very important. Why? Well, if you have young puppy, you know that it is one giant mouth that everything goes into. Sometimes valuable and dangerous things go in it. Stephen Hawking actually got the idea of the black hole from his puppy's ever-consuming mouth. If you teach your dog correctly, when you give the command "drop it!," he will open his mouth and drop whatever is in there, and most importantly he will allow you to retrieve it. When teaching the *drop it* command you must make a good trade for what your dog has in his mouth. You need to, *out treat* him, with a better treat of higher value than what he has in his mouth. In addition, it is a good idea to stay calm and not to chase your puppy. If you teach this command well, your puppy will eventually enjoy hearing the drop it commands. This command can also build trust. If you say, "drop it" and then you retrieve the item and afterwards treat your dog, your dog will know that you are not there to steal the things he finds. Because of the trust that will develop, he will *not guard* his favorite toys or food.

Teach "Drop It!" Like This

- Gather good treats, the top-notch stuff, and a few items your dog might like to chew on; toys, rawhide, or your dogs favorite. With treats in hand, encourage your dog to chew on one of the items. When it is in his mouth, *put the treat close to his nose* and say, "drop it!" As soon as he opens his mouth, treat him as you pick up the item. Then return the item to him. Now, your dog may not want to chew the item because there are treats in the area and want his mouth free for treats. That is fine. Keep the treats handy, and throughout the day when you see him pick something up, practice the *drop it* command. Do this at least ten times per day. In the event that he picks up a forbidden item, like Uncle Clumpy's wooden leg, you may not want to give it back to him. That's fine, but remember to give him an extra tasty treat, take the leg away, and wipe the drool off before returning it to Uncle Clumpy.

- Once you have done this treat to the nose *drop it* command ten times, try it without the treat to the nose. Say the command and when he drops the item, give him a treat from your pocket or pouch. Make sure you give him extra treats the first time he drops it without the treat to his nose.

- Once you have done the above ten to twelve times, you can next move forward giving your dog something more special, like a hard chew pig ear or rawhide, but avoid the half of roast ox as it might spoil his dinner. Next, hold this new chewy in your hand and offer it to him but *do not let it go*. When your dog has the chewy in his mouth say the "drop it" command. Give him extra treats the first time he drops it and then offer the chew again. Repeat the exercise. Again, because better treats are available, he may not take the chewy back. This is a good sign, but indicates a time for a break. Later, return to the training and repeat it about a dozen times before you move on to the next phase of "drop it!"

- Now, repeat the exercise above, but this time do not hold onto the chew, just let him have it. As soon as your dog has it in his mouth, give the command "drop it!" When he drops it, give the treat *and* give the chew back to him to keep. He will be thrilled. During this exercise, if he does not drop it, show the treat first, if necessary, and then work up to having him drop it before the treat appears. This in actuality is *bribery*, and I do not suggest doing this type of intervention on a regular basis nor do I suggest utilizing this action elsewhere during training. Use this method as a last resort, not as a short cut.

- Once you have done this ten times successfully, try the command with the things around the house he is not supposed to chew on, such as toilet paper, chip bags, pens, gloves, your shoes and that 15th century Guttenberg bible.

Then, try this exercise outside where there are plenty of distractions. Be sure and gather up the best treats when working outside, and keep moving into further distracting situations. Your goal is to have the *drop it* commands obeyed in any situation.

Know These Things-

- If your puppy already likes to grab things and have you chase him, start by teaching him that you will *not* go chasing him. If he grabs and runs, ignore him. He will get bored and drop the item on his own. *Remember ignoring means sight, sound, and body language.*

- If your dog will not drop an item, you can manually retrieve the item by placing your fingers on the lips of your dog's upper jaw. Attempt to calm your dog beforehand. Place your hand over the top of your dogs muzzle; apply even pressure on the upper lips by using your index and thumb fingers and pressing inwards into his teeth. In most cases, your dog will open its mouth to avoid having his lips pinched and you can retrieve the item in question, which might be a dead bird, dried dog poop, or an antibiotic. This may take a couple of practices to get the pressure and spot correct. If all fails you can use both hands and try to separate the jaw by pulling, not jerking, the upper and lower jaw apart.

- Try the command "drop it," while playing fetch games.

~ Paws On – Paws Off ~

"Leave it" Important for Living

 "Leave it" is a different command than "drop it!" The goal of the "leave it" command is to get your dog's attention away from any object before it is in his mouth. This will keep him safe from dangerous objects, such as dropped medications, glass, wires, or food of yours on the floor. Teach the "leave it" command as soon as your dog recognizes his own name.

- Start with a treat in each fisted hand. Let him have a sniff of one of your fists. When he eventually looks away from the fist and has stopped trying to get the treat, give him the treat. Treat your dog from the *other* hand. Repeat this exercise until he refrains from trying to get the treat from your fist.

- Now, open your hand with the treat in it and then show him. Close your hand if he tries to get the treat. Do this until he simply ignores the treat in the open hand, known as the decoy hand. When he ignores it, give him the treat from the *other* hand. Keep doing this until he ignores the treat in the open hand from start of the exercise. When you have reached this point, add the command "leave it". Now, open the decoy hand, say "leave it" just once for each repetition, and then treat him from the other hand.

- Now put the treat on the floor and say, "leave it". Cover it with your hand if he tries to get it. Treat him from the other hand when he looks away from the treat on the floor. Repeat this until he does not try to get the treat on the floor once you have given the command "leave it". Repeat this 6-10 times.

- Now, try the following steps. Put the treat on the floor, and say, "leave it" and then you stand up. Give a treat if he obeys. Now, walk him by the treat while on his leash, and say, "leave it" If he goes for it, prevent him from getting it by restraining him with the leash. Treat him when he ignores the treat. Increase the length of time between the "leave it" command and the treat. Teaching him to leave it with a treat first will allow you to build up to objects such as toys, animals, and people. You can build up to more and more difficult items with ease once he gets the idea in his head that leave it, means good rewards for him.

- After your dog is successful at leaving the treat and other items, take the training outside into the yard. Next, head to the dog park and then other places with distractions. Remember to keep your puppy clear of dog parks until at least after seven weeks and after his first round of vaccines. Continue practicing daily until your dog has it down pat. This is another potential life saving command.

~ *Paws On – Paws Off* ~

Let's Sit

Teaching your Bully to *sit* establishes human leadership shaping him to understand who the boss is, and it will be a perfect substitute command for other problem behaviors like jumping up on people. He will know what to do right away. Teaching him to sit is easy too.

- Find a quiet place and get your treats together. Wait until your dog sits down by his own will. As soon as his fuzzy rump hits the floor, give him a treat. Feed him while he is still sitting and then get him up and standing again. Continue doing this until your dog is sitting right away after you reward treat him for sitting.

- Now, say, "sit" and as he begins to sit, give him a treat. From here on, only treat him when he sits after being told to do so.

Try these variations for better sitting behavior:

- Practice five minutes a day in places with more and more distractions.

- Run around with your dog, play with a toy, and then ask him to sit. Reward him well when he does.

- Ask your dog to sit before you give him stuff he likes, such as going outside, food, toys, and petting.

- Get him to sit in a variety of situations, such as when strangers are around, when there is food on the table, outdoors, in the park, before opening doors, and so forth. Keep practicing in all situations you encounter. Sit is a powerful command, and will be useful for the life of your dog.

~ Paws On – Paws Off ~

Supine Time (Lie Down)

Teaching your Bully to lie down helps to keep him in one spot, calms him down, and it is a useful action to supersede barking.

Basics – "Down!"

- Find that quiet place and bring plenty of treats. Wait for your dog to lie down of his own will and then give him a treat while he is lying down. Toss a treat to get him up again. Keep doing this until he lies down directly after he gets the second treat. This means that your dog is starting to understand that good things come to him when he lies down so he is lying right back down.

- Now, as soon as he starts to lie down say "down," and treat him. From here on, only treat him when lies down on your command.

- Next, practice this in other places, for instance in areas with different distraction, around strangers, when wearing a hat, or wherever you happen to be when out. Be patient in the more distracting locations. It is wonderful when doggie accompanies you to the local morning coffee café, a place where you need your dog to lie quietly beside you whilst you drink your morning coffee. Delightful!

PROBLEMS SOLVED

- If he will not lie down, a good location for teaching him is in the bathroom. Unless your dog likes decorative bath soaps, and he may, there is not much to distract him in the bathroom.

- If he does lie down but pops right back up, be sure to treat him when in the lying down position. This way he will be quicker to understand the correlation between the command, action, and treat.

~ *Paws On – Paws Off* ~

"Stay," Right There Mister

 Self-control has practical uses such as keeping him from running out the door, jumping on people or the good behavior of waiting for you. "Stay" is a great command to teach your dog. This is an easy command to teach after you have taught him "sit" and "down" and they make a perfect pairing.

- Find yourselves a quiet place with plenty of treats at hand. Give the "sit" command, but wait two-seconds before you treat him. Continue this until he will sit for duration of ten seconds before he receives a treat. *Begin to use the phrase "sit- stay"when* issuing a command. At the stay part, add a hand signal. This signal should be your flat hand towards your dog at about a foot or so from his fuzzy little face.

- If he gets up, it means you are moving too quickly. Try again with a shorter stay time goal, and then gradually increase the time for your dog to stay.

- Say "sit-stay" and take one big step away from your dog, then treat him for staying. Keep going until you can take two steps in any direction away from him without him moving. Make sure you go back to him to treat each time he stays. *If he comes to you, do not treat him.*

- Keep doing this until you can take several steps and eventually move out of sight with your dog staying in place. Work until you can get him to stay for a two full minutes while you are in his sight, then two or more minutes out of your dog's sight.

- Now, try all this starting with the "down" command.

HELPFUL HINTS

- Vary the difficulty; your dog might decide not to participate if it keeps getting harder and harder all the time.

- *Always*, reward him where he stayed. Do not release him with a "come" command and then treat him. Keep it clear and simple and do not add extra commands to this training.

Practice "stay" regularly before you give him his food bowl, before he meets a new person, before he goes out the door or when he goes on that big night out.

~ *Paws On – Paws Off* ~

Going Out On a Leash Here

Training your dog to the leash is probably one of the hardest things you will do. However, in the end, it is very rewarding and can strengthen the trust and bond between  you and your dog. There is a variety of collars to choose from, so do some research, and figure out which one is best for your dog. Head collars and front attachment harnesses are a couple of choices. Make sure it fits right, the leash is not too long, he is comfortable in it, and is stylish enough so the other dogs will not mock him. The main goal here is to get your dog to walk beside you without pulling against the leash. An easy way to prevent that is to stop moving forward when he pulls, and then to reward him with treats when he walks beside you. The following steps will help you train your dog to have excellent leash manners. Loose leash walking is the goal.

Walking With You Is A Treat (The beginning)

Put a non-retractable leash on your dog, ten to 20 feet long. Load up with top-notch treats and head out to the back yard or a familiar, quiet outdoor spot. Decide whether you want your dog to walk on your left or ride side, and it is at this side you choose that you will always treat him, at thigh level. Soon, your dog will automatically be coming to that side because that is where the treats can be found. Later you can train your dog to behave the same on the opposite side you choose now. This allows you do walk your dog out of way of the traffic or danger no matter where you are walking.

Start walking randomly around the yard. When your dog decides to walk with you, give him a treat at thigh level of your chosen side. To "walk with you" refers to an appropriate action where you begin to move and your dog walks along with you, not pulling in a different direction. If he continues to walk with you on the correct side, give him a treat with every step or two that you take together. Keep practicing this until your dog is staying by your side more often than not. Do not worry about the treats; you will eventually faze them out when he learns this behavior.

Eyes on the THIGHS (Second act)

Start walking around the yard again and wait for your dog to lag behind or get distracted by something else. Say, "let's go" to him and slap your thigh to get his attention. Make sure you use a cheerful, welcoming tone. When he pays attention to you, walk away.

- If he catches up with you before the leash gets tight, treat him from your thigh on the chosen side. Treat him again after he takes a couple of steps with you.

- If he catches up after the leash gets tight do not treat him, then say, "let's go" again and treat him after he takes a couple of steps with you.

- If he does not come when you say, "let's go" and as the leash gets tight, stop walking and apply some gentle pressure to the leash. When he begins to come toward you praise him. When he gets to you, do not treat him, rather say, "let's go" again. Treat him if he stays with you and keep treating him for every step or two he stays with you.

- Keep practicing this step until he is staying at your side while you walk around the yard. If he moves away from you say, "let's go" to redirect him, and then treat him.

Oh the things to smell and pee on (Third act)

Just like you, your dog is going to want to sniff things and go potty. When he is on the leash, every five minutes or so, when you would normally treat him, say, "go sniff," "go play," "free time," or something like that. Then, let him have some free time on the leash. Keep in mind this is a form of reward so if he pulls on the leash during this time say, "let's go" and walk the opposite direction, ending free time quickly and cleanly.

Where's the BOSS? (Fourth act)

Continue practicing leash walking in the yard using steps one through three. Gradually, shorten the leash until you have about a 6-foot length. Change direction, change speed, and treat him every time he is able to stay with you during the changes. Now, when he is used to walking by your side you can start phasing out the treats, except continue to treat him when he does something difficult like keeping up with the changes.

Out in the Streets (Fifth act)

Now take your dog out of the back yard and onto the sidewalk for his daily walk. You will apply the same techniques you used in your back yard, only now you have to deal with more distractions. Now, you will be dealing with other dogs, friendly strangers, squirrels, traffic, and who knows what else. Arm yourself with the special treats, be patient, and go slow. Use the "let's go" command when he pulls his leash or forgets that you exist. Give him treats when he walks beside you. Moreover, do not forget *sniff breaks*, those are rewards too.

Stop and Go exercise (Sixth act)

 Have a 6-foot leash attached to the collar. Hold the leash and toss a treat or toy about twenty feet ahead and start walking toward it. If he pulls the leash and tries to get the treat, use the "let's go" command and walk in the opposite direction of the treat. If he stays beside you while you walk toward the treat let him have it as his reward. Practice this several times until he no longer pulls toward the treat but stays at your side. Remember you should be in control of sniffing and potty stops

TROUBLE SHOOTING

- If your dog is crossing in front of you make your presence known to him. He may be distracted.

- If he is lagging behind you, he might be frightened or not feeling well. Give him a lot of encouragement instead of pulling him along. If the lagging is due to sniffing or frequent potty breaks, keep walking. In this case, apply only gentle pressure to the leash.

- Remember to give lots, and lots, of rewards when he walks beside you.

Heel

This is a good command to teach your dog when you encounter distractions, such as other dogs, traffic, construction danger, or just about anything, that warrants keeping your dog close to you so he does not get into trouble or danger. The heel command is to let your dog know that he needs to come and remain close beside you while walking until you say otherwise.

- Begin this in your back yard or low distraction area. First, place a treat in your fist on the chosen side of your body. Let him sniff the fist and say "heel" then, take a few steps leading him along with the treat in your fist at thigh level. Treat him when he is following your fist with his nose.

- Next, say "heel" and have him follow at your side with an empty fist. When he follows your fist for a couple of steps treat him. Practice this for half dozen or more repetitions.

- Continue to practice heel, but now increase the length of time before you treat him, moving around, changing direction or some new maneuver.

- Now, try this outside of your back yard and in more distracting situations.

Continue to practice this command each time you take your dog out on the leash. Keeping it fresh will ease your mind because you will know that your dog will comply when necessary. Out in the crazy, nutty, world of ours there are plenty of instances when you will use this command to avoid unnecessary confrontations or circumstances. If you choose to use a different command other than heel pick a word that is uncommon in everyday language, such as "cactus," "pickle," or "zing".

~   *Paws   On   —   Paws   Off*   ~

"Go" West Young Bully

"Go" is a great cue to get your Bully into his crate, into the car, or off the couch. This is a very handy command to send your dog to a specific location.

- Find a quiet place, have treats, and bring your dog. Place a towel or mat on the floor. Put a treat in your hand and use it to lure your dog onto the towel while saying, "Go". When all four paws are on the towel, give him a treat. Do this about ten times.

- Start the same way as above, but this time be empty-handed. When all four paws are on the towel, treat him while on the towel. Do this ten times.

- Keep practicing with an empty hand and eventually turning the empty hand into a pointed index finger. Do this about ten times.

- Now, cue with "go" *while pointing* to the towel, but do not walk to the towel with him.

- Now, try this on different surfaces and other places, such as different rooms, houses, grass, tile, and carpet. Continue to practice this in more and more distracting situations and don't forget your towel or mat.

One Step Beyond – Settle

This is an extra command you can teach. The purpose is to teach your dog to go to a mat and lie on it until he is released. This is for when you need your dog out from under foot for extended lengths of time. Pair it with down and stay so your dog will go the mat and lie down.

- Place a mat on the floor. An actual mat, not your neighbor named Matt, even though tempting.

- Give the "go" command and treat him when he has all four paws on the mat. While he is on the mat, issue the command, "down – stay" Go to him and treat while on the mat.

- Now, give the "Settle" cue and repeat the above exercise.

- Give the "settle" cue and wait for him to go to the mat and lie down before you treat him. Do not use any other cues at this time.

- Make it more difficult; vary the distance, add distractions, and increase the times in the settle mode.

~ Paws On – Paws Off ~

Jumping Jeepers

Your dog loves you and wants as much attention from you as possible. The reality is that you are the world to him. If he is sitting quietly, he is easily forgotten. When he is walking beside you, you are probably thinking about other things, such as work, the car, or anything but your loyal companion lying next to you. He gets your full attention only when he jumps up on you. Then you look at him, maybe shout at him, and gently push him down until he is down on the floor. Then, you ignore him again. What do you expect? He wants your attention. Teaching your dog not to jump is essentially teaching him that attention will come only if he has all fours on the floor.

Now, it is important not to punish your dog when teaching him not to jump up on you and others. Do not shout "no!" or "bad!" Do not knee him or push him. The best way to handle the jumping is to turn your back and ignore him. Remember, since he loves you very much, your dog or puppy may take any physical contact from you as a positive sign. You do not want to send mixed signals; instead, you want to practice complete ignoring that consists of no looking or audio.

For jumping practice, it would be ideal if you could gather a group of people. You want to train your dog to understand that he will only get attention if he is on the ground. If groups of people are not available, then teach him to remain grounded using his family. When he encounters other people, use a strong "sit - stay" command to keep all four paws planted firmly on the ground.

No Jumping On the Family

This is the easiest part because the family and frequent visitors have more chances to help your dog or puppy to learn. When you come in from outside and your dog starts jumping up, say, "oops!" and immediately leave through the same door. Wait a few seconds after leaving and then do it again. When he finally stops jumping upon you as you enter, give him a lot of attention. Ask the rest of the family to follow the same protocol when they come into the house. If you find that he is jumping up at other times as well, like when you sing karaoke, just ignore him by turning your back and put energy into giving him attention when he is sitting.

No Jumping on Others

Prevention is the key to this exercise, especially with larger dogs. You can prevent him from jumping by using a leash, a tieback, crate, and gate. Until you have had enough practice and your dog knows what you want him to do, you really should use one of these methods to prevent him from hurting someone or getting an inadvertent, petting reward for jumping. To train, you will need to go out and solicit some dog training volunteers and infrequent visitors to help.

Guests Who Want to Help Train Your Dog (Thank you in advance)

- At home, a guest comes in through the door, the dog jumps up, they are to say "oops" and leave immediately. Practice this with at least five different visitors, each making multiple entrances during the same visit. If your helpers are jumped, have them completely ignore your dog.

- When on the streets, have your dog on a leash. Have the guest approach your dog. If he strains against the leash or jumps, the guest turns their back and walks away. When your dog calms himself and sits, the guest approaches again. Repeat this until the guest can approach, pet and give attention to your dog without your dog jumping up. Have the volunteer repeat this at least five times.

- Make what is called a "tieback," which is a leash attached to something sturdy, within site of the doorway but not blocking the entrance. Keep this there for a few months during training. When the guest arrives, hook your dog to the secure leash and then, let the guest in.

- Once your dog is calm, the visitor can greet him if they wish. If the guest does not wish to greet your dog, give your dog a treat to calm his behavior. If he barks, send him to his crate or the gated time out area. The goal is that you always greet your guests first, *not your dog*.

- If he is able to greet guests calmly while tied back, then he may be released. At first hold the leash to see how your dog reacts, then if he is calm release him.

A Caveat to These Two Methods

1) Teach your dog that grabbing your left shoulder means the same as the command "sit." By combining the word "sit" with a hand on left shoulder, he will learn this. If you want to use another physical cue, you can substitute your

own gesture here. Ask your guests, the ones who want to help train him, to put their right hand on their left shoulders and wait until your dog sits before they pet him or give any attention. Training people that meet your dog will help both you and your dog in preventing unwanted excitement and jumping up.

2) For those who are not volunteers to help teach your dog and are at your home visiting, there is another method. Always keep treats by the door and toss them when someone comes in. Toss treats six to ten feet away from that visiting person. Your dog of pup will eventually anticipate this and will stay away and off the person. When he has calmed down a bit, ask him to sit and then, give him some good attention.

~ *Paws On – Paws Off* ~

Barking Madness

Dogs bark for many reasons, most commonly, for attention. Your Bully may bark because he wants to play or when he wants you to feed him. Whatever the case, *don't do it*. Do not give your dog attention for barking. Say, "leave it" and ignore him. *You* do not want him to learn that barking works to get you moving. While not looking at him go to the other side of the room. Make it clear to your barking dog that his barking does not result in any rewards or attention. In the end, make sure you are initiating activities he likes and make them happen on *your* schedule. You are the alpha leader so regularly show your pup who is in charge. Also, make sure that he earns what he gets. Have your pup *sit* before he gets the reward of going outside to play, getting his leash put on, his bowl of food, or loaded into the car to go tailgating

Your dog may bark when seeing or hearing something interesting. Below are a few ways to deal with this issue.

When you are at your residence

- *Prevent it*. Block the source of sound or sight. Use a fan or blinds, or simply put him in a different area of the house to keep him from the stimulus.

- *Teach him quiet*. When your dog barks, wave a piece of food in front of his nose. When he stops barking to sniff, treat him right away. After doing this about three times, the next time he barks, pretend you have a piece of food and say, "quiet." Always treat him as soon as he *stops* barking. After issuing the "quiet" command, treat him again for every few seconds that he remains quiet. Eventually, you can increase the time lapses between cues and treats.

- When your pup hears or sees something that would usually make him bark and he doesn't bark, reward him.

The Time Out

You can use a "time-out" but do not use it too often. When you give your dog a time out, you are taking him out of his social circle and giving him what is known as a negative punishment. This kind of punishment can have side effects that you do not want. Side effects can include learning that the action of you walking towards him is a bad thing. The *time out* should be used very sparingly and to emphasize the teaching of your dog the behavior that you prefer while preventing the bad behavior.

- Choose a place where you want the time out spot to be. Make sure that this place is not the potty spot, the play area, or the Saturday night square dancing spot. It should be somewhere that is not scary, not too comfortable, but safe. A gated pantry or the bathroom can work well. If your puppy does not mind his crate, you can use it. Secure a 2-foot piece of rope or a short leash to your puppy's collar. When your pup barks, use a calm voice and give the command, "time out," then take the rope and walk him firmly but gently to the time out spot. Leave him there for about 5 minutes. When he is calm and not barking you can release him. You may need to do this few times before he understands which behavior has put him into the time out.

When you are away from your residence

- Again, prevent barking by blocking the sounds or sights that are responsible for setting your dog or puppy off into barking mode. Use a fan, blinds or keep him in another part of the house away from the stimulus.

- Use a Citronella Spray Collar. Only use this for when the barking become intolerable. Do not use this when the barking is associated with fear or aggression. You will want to use this a few times when you are at home, so he understands how it works.

Citronella collars work like this. The collar has a sensitive microphone, which senses when your dog is barking, when this happens it triggers a small release of citronella spray into the area above a dog's nose. It surprises the dog and disrupts barking by and emitting a smell that dog's dislike.

Out walking

While you are out walking your dog, from excitement your dog might bark at other dogs, people, cars, and critters out of shear excitement.

Here are some helpful tools to defuse that behavior.

- Teach him the *watch me* command. Begin this training in the house where there are fewer distractions. Say your dog's name and "watch me" while you hold a treat to your nose. Treat him when he looks at the treat for at least one second.

- First, practice the treat to the nose "watch me" with a treat ten times, and then repeat while pretending to have a treat on your nose. You will then want to incorporate this hand to your nose as your hand signal for *watch me*.

- Build the duration of time that your dog can continue to watch you without fuss.

- Now, practice the "watch me" command while you are walking around inside the house. Then practice this again outside. When outside, practice near something he finds interesting. Practice in a situation he would normally bark. Continue practicing in different situations and other catalyst that set your dog off barking.

Other Solutions

The *quiet* command is for when your dog begins to bark, or when you notice something that would make him bark, prior to him barking. For example, when the bark trigger, the skateboarder that zooms by your house daily comes zooming by. Use the command *quiet* and give him a treat. Treat him every for every few seconds that he remains quiet. Teach him that the trigger of his gets him a "quiet" command. If he frequently barks while a car is passing by, put a treat by his nose, and then bring it to your nose. When he looks at you, treat him. Repeat this until he voluntarily looks at you when a car goes by and does not bark, continuing to *treat* him appropriately.

 - You can also treat him for calm behavior. When you see something or encounter something that he would normally bark at and he does not, treat him.

- If you are out walking and your dog has not yet learned the quiet cue, or is not responding to it, turn around and walk away from whatever is causing your dog to bark. When he calms down, offer a treat.

- Use the citronella spray collar if your dogs barking cannot be controlled using the techniques that you have learned. Use this only when the barking is *not* associated with fear or aggression.

Your dog is Afraid, Aggressive, Lonely, Territorial, or Hung-over

Your dog may have outbursts when he feels any of these things. You should first try to prevent outbursts by crating, gating, blocking windows, using fans to hide sounds and avoid taking him places that can cause these outbursts. This is not a permanent solution, but is a helpful solution when you are teaching. To allow your dog a chance to find his center, relax his mind and body, you want to do this for about seven days before beginning to train against barking.

SOME TIPS

- Always, remain calm, because a relaxed and composed alpha achieves great training outcomes.

- If training is too stressful, you may want to hire a professional positive trainer for private sessions. "When doing so, tell him or her, to first read my eBook, and then follow it closely, (wink)."

It is important to help your dog to modify his thinking about what tends to upset him. Teach him that, what he was upset about before now predicts his favorite things. Here is how.

- When the trigger appears in the distance, treat him. Keep treating him as you get him closer to the negative stimulus. If he is territorially aggressive, teach him that the doorbell or a knock on the door means it is his cue to get into his crate and wait for treats. You can do this by ringing the doorbell and luring him to his crate and giving him treats.

- You can also lure him through his fears. If you are out walking and encounter one of his triggers, put a treat to his nose and lead him out and away from the trigger zone.

- Use the "watch me" command when you see him getting nervous or afraid. Treat him frequently for watching you.

- Reward *calm* behavior.

Your dog is frustrated, bored or both

Your dog or puppy may get bored or frustrated because he can sense he is not making you happy. At these times, your dog may lose focus, not pay attention to you, and spend time writing bad poetry in his journal. Here are a few things that can help prevent this:

- Keep him busy and tire him out with chew toys, exercise, play, and training.

- He should have at least 30 minutes of aerobic exercise per day. In addition to the aerobic exercise, he should have 1 hour of chewing and about 15 minutes of training. Keep it interesting for him with a variety of activities. It is, after all, the spice of life.

Excited to Play

Like an actor in the wings, your puppy will get excited about play. Teach him that when he starts to bark, the play stops. Put a short leash on him and if he barks, use it to lead him out of play sessions. Put him in a time out or just stop playing with him. Reward him with more play when he calms down.

~ Paws On – Paws Off ~

The Ole Nipperdoggie

Friendly puppies nip for a few reasons; they are teething, playing or they want to get your attention. My Uncle Dexter nips from a bottle, but that is a completely different story. Not to worry, in time most puppies will grow out of this behavior naturally. Other herding dogs nip as a herding instinct. They do this to round up their animal charges or family members.

While he is working through the nipping stage, you will want to avoid punishing or correcting your dog, as this could eventually result in a strained relationship down the road. You also want to teach your puppy how delicate human skin is. Let him test it out and give him feedback. Say 'ylpe!', 'youch!', or 'bowie!' and pull your hand back when he nips too hard. If you act more and more sensitive to the nips, he will understand the fact that humans are very sensitive and will respond accordingly.

This is a very easy behavior to modify because we know the motivation behind it. The puppy wants to play and chew and who doesn't? Give your dog access to a variety of chew toys, and when he nips, walk away and ignore him. If he follows you, and nips at your heels, give your dog a time out. Afterward, when he is relaxed and gentle, stay and play with him. Use the utmost in patience with your puppy. In time this will pass.

Preventing the Nippage

- Have a chew toy in your hand when you are playing with your puppy. This way he learns what the right thing is to bite and chew, and it is not your hand.

- Get rid of your puppy's excess energy by exercising him *at least* an hour each day. As a result, he will have no energy to nip.

- Make sure he is getting enough rest and he is not cranky. Twelve hours per day is good for dogs, and as it seems for teenagers as well.

- Always have lots of interesting chew toys available to help your puppy through the teething process.

- Children should not be left unsupervised when around dogs and puppies. Also, teach your kids not to run away screaming from nipping puppies. They should walk away quietly or simply stay still.

Instructing Around the Nippage

- Play with him and praise him for being gentle. When he nips say, "*yipe!*" like a puppy would say and quickly walk away.

- After the nipping, wait one minute and then return to give him another chance to play or just be in your presence without nipping. Practice this for two or three minutes and remember to give everyone who will have daily contact with the puppy, a chance to play and train him, as well.

- Use a tie-back to secure your pup or put him in a room with a baby gate or something that you can get over quickly. Use while your dog is under supervision.

- This method also works well for other attention getting behaviors like jumping, barking, and the dreaded leg humping.

~ *Paws On – Paws Off* ~

Housetraining the Pup

The fact is, dogs are a bit particular about where they "potty" and will invariably build a very strong habit. When house-training your puppy, remember that whenever he goes *potty somewhere* in the house, he is building a strong preference to that particular area. When your dog does relieve his self in the house, *blame yourself*. Until your puppy has learned where he is supposed to do his business, you should keep a constant, watchful eye on him, whether he is in his crate, on a mat or on the couch.

- If he is having accidents in the crate, it may be too big. The crate should be big enough to stand up, turn around, and lay down in.

- When he is inside, out of the crate, watch for sniffing or circling, and as soon as you see this behavior, take him out right away. Do not hesitate.

- Set a timer to go off every hour so that you remember to take him out before nature calls. With progress, you can increase the time duration between potty stops.

- If he does not do his *duty* when you taken out, bring him back in and keep a close eye, then try again in 15-minutes. Just like some humans, he might be shy.

Schedule This

You should take your puppy out many times during the day, most importantly after eating, playing, or sleeping. Feed him appropriate amounts of food two or three times per day and leave the food down for around 15-minutes at a time, then remove. Your younger dogs can generally hold for a good 1-hour stretch. Adult dogs generally do not go longer than 8 hours between potty breaks. In the beginning, frequently take your puppy outside frequently. This avoids accidents in the house and gives him more chances to receive rewards from you for doing what you want him to. You can keep his water down until about eight at night then remove it from your puppy's reach.

Consistency Is the Mother of Prevention

Until your puppy is reliably house-trained, bring him outside to the same spot each time, always leaving a little bit of his waste there as a scent marker. This will be the designated potty spot. Place a warning sign at that spot if you like. Remember to use this spot for potty only, and not for play. Bring your puppy to his spot and say something like "hurry up" when you see him getting ready to go. As he is going, say nothing, this will distract him. When he finishes, praise, pet, and give a top-notch treat. Spend about five minutes or so playing with him too, avoiding the potty spot. If he does not go, take him inside, keep an eye on him, and try again in 15 minutes.

If your puppy goes in the house, remember, that is *your fault*. Maybe you went too quickly with the training or were not clear enough about the potty spot. If you see your puppy relieving himself in the wrong spot, quickly bring him outside to the potty spot, when he is done, offer praise for finishing there. If you find a mess, clean it thoroughly without your puppy watching you do it. Use a cleaner specifically for pet stains so there is no smell or evidence that you failed him. This way it will not become a regular spot for him and a new regular clean up chore for you.

This Question Rings a Bell: Can I teach him when to tell me when he needs to go out?

Yes, you can! Hang a bell at dog level, beside the door you use to let your dog outdoors. Put some peanut butter on the bell. When he touches it and rings it, immediately open the door. Repeat this every time and take him to the potty spot. Eventually, he will ring the bell without the peanut butter and this will tell you when he needs to go outside. Be careful here, he may start to ring the bell when he wants to go outside to play, explore, or to go outside for non-potty reasons. To avoid this, each time he rings the bell, take him out to the potty spot *only*. If he starts to play, immediately bring him in the house.

Small Dogs often take longer time to potty train. I really do not know why, they just do. One way to help is to take them out more often than you would a larger dog. The longest duration I would go without taking a small dog to the potty spot is about 4 hours, and as a puppy maybe forty-five minutes instead of an hour. In addition, many small dogs do well with a litter box. This way, they can go whenever nature calls and whatever the situation is, such as when there is a blizzard outside and they refuse to get their tiny little paws cold. "Remember, your little pooch may be small, but do not call him 'kitty', as he will feel disrespected".

~ *Paws On – Paws Off* ~

Part III: Body Language and Vocals

Training your dog seems like a daunting task, but it is a unique and rewarding experience. It is the foundation of a healthy and long relationship with your new dog or puppy. You must be the one in charge of the relationship and lead with the pack leader mentality, all the while showing patience and love. Whether you choose to enroll your dog in an obedience school such as the Sirius reward training system or go it alone at home, you will the need assistance of quality books, videos, and articles to help guide you through the process and find solutions to obstacles along the way.

Without a doubt, it is nice to have an obedient friend by your side through good times and bad. Owning a dog is a relationship that needs tending throughout the years. Once you begin training, it will continue throughout the life of your dog and friend. An obedient dog is easier to care for and causes less household problems and expense. You know what needs to be done, but what about your dog. How do you read his messages in regards to what you are attempting to accomplish? I am going to cover dog's body language and vocal language to provide insight into what it is your dog Is trying to tell you. This should prove to be an asset while training your dog.

Body Language:

What is body language? Body language is all of the non-verbal communication we exhibit when engaged into an exchange with another entity. Say what? All of those little tics, spasms, and movements that we act out comprise of non-verbal body language. Studies state that over 50% of how people judge us is based on our use of body language. Apparently, the visual interpretation of our message is equal to our verbal message. It is interesting how some studies have indicated that when the body language disagrees with the verbal, our verbal message accounts for as little as 7-10% of how the others judge us. With that kind of statistic, I would say that body language is extremely important.

Similar to humans, dogs use their bodies to communicate. Their hearing and seeing senses are especially acute. Observe how your dog tilts his head, moves his legs, and what his tail is doing. Is the tail up, down, or wagging? These body movements are all part of the message your dog is trying to convey. With this knowledge, I think it is safe to say that we should learn a little about human and dog body language. In this article, I will stick to a dog's body language and leave the human investigation up to you. What do you think my posture is right now?

The Tail:

The tail is a wagging and this means the dog is friendly, or maybe not. With most dogs that have tails it can convey many messages, some nice, some nasty. Specialists say a dogs wagging tail can mean the dog is scared, confused, preparing to fight, confident, concentrating, interested, or happy.

How do you tell the difference? Look at the speed and range of motion in the tail. The wide-fast tail wag is usually the message of "Hey, I am so happy to see you!" wag. The tail that is not tight between the hind legs, but instead is sticking straight back horizontally means the dog is curious but unsure, and probably not going to bite but remain in a place of neutral affection. This dog will probably not be confrontational, yet the verdict is not in.

The slow tail wag means the same; the dog's friendly meter is gauging the other as friend or foe. The tail held high and stiff, or bristling (hair raised) is a WATCH OUT! Red Flag warning for humans to be cautious. This dog may not only be aggressive, but dangerous and ready to rumble. If you come across this dog, it is time to calculate your retreat and escape plan.

Not only should the speed and range of the wag be recognized while you are reading doggie body language, one must also take note of the tail position. A dog that is carrying its tail erect is a self-assured dog in control of itself. On the flip side of that, the dog with their tail between their legs, tucked in tight is the, "I surrender man, I surrender, please don't hurt me" posture. This following applies to humans as well as our fellow K-9's, is the chill dog, a la Reggae special. This is the dog that has her tail lowered but not tucked in-between her legs. The tail that is down and relaxed in a neutral position states, the dog is the also relaxed.

While training your dog or simply playing, it is a good idea to take note of what his or her tail is doing and determine if your dog's tail posture is matching their moods. Your understanding of your dog's tail movements and body posture will be of great assistance throughout its lifetime.

Up Front:

On the front end of the dog is the head and ears with their special motions. A dog that cocks her head or twitches her ears is giving the signal of interest and awareness, but sometimes it can indicate fear. The forward or ear up movements can show a dog's awareness of seeing or hearing something new. Due to the amazingly acute canine sense of hearing, this can occur long before we are aware. These senses are two of the assets that make dogs so special and make that make them fantastic watch guards.

"I give in, and will take my punishment" is conveyed with the head down and ears back. Take note of this submissive posture, observe the neck, and back fur for bristling. Sometimes this accompanies this posture. Even though a dog is giving off this submissive stance, it should be approached with caution because it may feel threatened and launch an offensive attack thinking he needs to defend himself.

"Smile, you are on camera." Yep, you got it, dogs smile too. It is usually a subtle corner pull back to show the teeth. Do not confuse this with the obvious snarl that entails a raised upper lip and bared teeth, sometimes accompanied by a deep growling sound. The snarl is something to be extremely cautious of when encountered. A snarling dog is not joking around-- *the snarl is serious*. This dog is ready to 'throw down'.

The Whole Kit and Caboodle:

Using the entire body, a dog that rolls over onto her back and exposes her belly, neck, and genitals is conveying the message that you are in charge. A dog that is overly submissive sometimes will urinate a small amount to express her obedience towards a human or another dog.

Front paws down, rear end up, tail is a waggin.' This, "hut, hut, hut, C'mon Sparky hike the ball," posture is the ole K-9 position of choice for, "Hey! it is playtime, and I am ready to go!" This posture is sometimes accompanied with a playful bark and or pawing of the ground in an attempt to draw you into her playful state. I love it when a dog is in this mood, albeit they can be aloof to commands.

Whines, Growls, Howls, Barks and Yelps. Sounds Dog's Make and We Hear

We just had a look at the silent communication of body language. Now, I will look into the doggie noises we cherish, but sometimes find annoying. Just what is our dog trying to tell us? Our K-9 friends often use vocal expressions to get their needs met. Whines and growls mean what they say, so when training your dog, listen carefully. As you become accustomed to the dogs vocal communication, and are able to begin understanding them, the happier you will both become. Some dog noises can be annoying and keep you awake, or wake you up. This may need your attention, to be trained out as inappropriate vocalizations.

Barking:

What does a dog bark say and why bark at all? Dogs bark to say "Hey, what's up dude" or "Look at me!" A bark may warn of trouble, or to convey that the dog is bored and or lonely. I think we all know that stimulated and excited dogs also bark. It is up to us to survey the surroundings and assess the reason. We need to educate ourselves about our dog's various barks so we can act appropriately.

Whining and Whimpering:

Almost from the time they are freshly made and feeding upon their mother's milk, our little puppies begin to make their first little fur-ball noises. Whimpering or whining to get their mothers attention for feeding or comfort is innate, and as a result, they know mom will come to them. They also use these two W's on us to gain our attention, as well. Other reasons for whimpering or whining are from fear produced by loud noises such as thunderstorms or fireworks. I think most of us have experienced the 4th of July phenomenon where the entire dog population is going at it until the wee hours of the morning when the last fireworks are ignited, and the final "BOOM!" dies off.

Growl:

Growling means, you had better watch out. Be acutely aware of what this dog is doing or might do. Usually a dog that is growling is seriously irritated and preparing to be further aggressive.

Howl:

Picture the dark silhouette of a howling dog with a full moon backdrop. A dog's howl is a distinct vocalization that most dogs use, and every wolf makes. Howling can mean loneliness, desire, warning, or excitement. A lonely howl is a dog looking for a response. Dogs also howl after a long hunt when they have tracked and cornered their prey.

A Couple of Things Regarding Training Your Dog:

Knowing what you want to train your dog to do is as important as training your dog. A puppy is a blank slate and knows no rules, so it is a good idea to make a list and have an understanding of what you would like your puppy to do. As he grows, the same principle applies and you may adjust training from the basics to further topics like making a good travel, hiking, or hunting dog. The conditions that you plan to expose your dog or puppy to outside of the household may require different training tactics as well as exposure to circumstances and environments that will allow him to be ready for those encounters.

Important Things to Remember In Training:

There is no such thing as starting too early. *Do not hit or yell at your dog.* Timing is crucial. Rewarding needs to be made promptly. Patience and consistency are your allies in the training game. From the beginning, establish yourself as the pack leader. You are the alpha and pledge to provide and properly care for your dog or puppy.

Please be kind and patient with your pets and dogs, but remember that *you are in charge and you need to lead with confidence.*

~ Paws On – Paws Off ~

Basic Care, Dog and Human Goals

Chow Time

- Low Quality Foods: Stay away from corn, wheat, by products, artificial preservatives, and artificial colors. Also, avoid anything in the 'eetos' food group, such as Cheetos, Doritos, burritos, and mosquitoes.

- Avoid junk food, period. It also helps if you do not teach your dog how to use your cell phone and order a pizza. Consult your veterinarian if you think you need specific diet guidance for your dog.

Handling

- Your Dog needs to be comfortable being touched on paws, ears, tail, mouth, entire body, and this should be practiced daily.

Basic Care

Oral maintenance, clipping, and other grooming will depend upon you and your dog's activities. We all know our dogs love to roll and run through all sorts of possible ugly messes, and put obscene things into their mouths, then afterward run up to lick us. Below is a list of the basic grooming care your dog requires. Pick up a grooming book on your specific breed so that you know what and how often your dog needs particular services, extra care areas, and what you may need to have done by professionals.

Most basic care can easily be done at home by you, but if you are unsure or uncomfortable about something, get some tutelage and in no time you will be clipping, trimming, and brushing like a professional.

Coat Brushing - Daily brushing of your dogs coat can be done, or a minimum of 4-5 times a week depending upon your breed's coat. Some breeds blow their coat once or twice a year and daily brushing is recommended during this period. Many breeds do not require daily brushing but it is still healthy for the coat and skin.

Some Equipment: Longhaired dogs need pin brushes,  short, medium, and some longhaired dogs need bristle brushes. Slicker brushes remove mats and dead hair. Rubber Curry Combs polish smooth coats. There are clippers, stripping knives, rakes, and more or less depending upon your dog's coat.

Bathing - Regular but not frequent bathing is essential. Much depends upon your breed's coat. Natural coat oils are needed to keep your dogs coat and skin moisturized. Never bathe your dog too frequently. Depending upon what your dog has been into, a bath once month is adequate. Bathing should be done at least once per month, with plenty of warm water and a gentle shampoo or soap made for dogs.

Nail trimming – For optimal foot health, your dog's nails should be kept short. There are special clippers that are needed for nail trimming that are designed to avoid injury. You can start trimming when your dog is a puppy, and you should have no problems. However, if your dog still runs for the hills or squirms like an eel at trimming time, then your local groomer or veterinarian can do this procedure.

Ear cleaning – You should clean your dog's ears at least once a month depending upon your breed, but be sure to inspect them every few days for bugs such as mites and ticks. Also, look for any odd discharge which can be an indication of infection and that its time for a visit to the vet. Remember to clean the outer ear only, by using a damp cloth or a cotton swab doused with mineral oil.

Eye cleaning - Use a moist cotton ball to clean any discharge from the eye. Avoid putting anything irritating around or into your dog's eyes.

Brushing teeth - Pick up a specially designed canine tooth brush and cleaning paste. Clean your dog's teeth as frequently as daily. Try to brush your dog's teeth a few times a week at a minimum. If your dog wants no part of having his or her teeth brushed, try rubbing his teeth and gums with your finger. After he is comfortable with this, you can now put some paste on your finger, allowing him to smell and lick it, then repeat rubbing his teeth and gums with your finger. Then, you may want to repeat with the brush now that he's comfortable with your finger. In addition, it's important to keep plenty of chews around to promote the oral health of your pooch. When your dog is 2-3 years old, he or she may need their first professional teeth cleaning.

Anal sacs - These sacs are located on each side of a dog's anus. If you notice your dog scooting his rear, or frequently licking and biting at his anus, the anal sacs may be impacted. You can ask your veterinarian how to diagnose and treat this issue.

Doing Things: Fun and Educational

- To avoid doggy boredom, make sure you have plenty of toys for your dog to choose from out of the toy bin. A Nylabone™, a Kong™, dog chews, ropes, balls, and tugs are many of the popular things your dog can enjoy. Your more advanced breeds might enjoy mahjong, air hockey, or play station. Please limit their time playing video games.

Be sure your dog is:

- Comfortable with human male and female adults.

- Comfortable with human male and female children.

- Comfortable with special circumstance people, for example, those in wheel chairs, with crutches, braces, or even strange "Uncle Larry."

To assure that your dog isn't selfish, make sure that he or she is:

- Comfortable with his food bowl, toys or bed being touched by you or others.

- Comfortable sharing the immediate space with strangers, especially with children. This is necessary of his socialization so that he doesn't get paranoid or freak out in small places. For example, elevators in Hollywood filled with celebrities and their handbags, or next-door neighbor's house.

- Comfortable sharing his best friend, YOU, and all family members and friends.

For road trippn' with your dog, make sure he or she is:

- Comfortable in a car, truck, minivan, or in a form of public transportation.

- Always properly restrained.

- Knows how to operate a stick shift as well as an automatic.

In general, a happy puppy should have the following:

- You should provide at least 10 hours of sleep per night for your dog. This should occur in one of the household's adult bedrooms, but not in the bed. He or she should have their own bed or mat available to them.

- Regular health checks at the vet are essential. He or she should receive at least the basic vaccinations, which includes rabies and distemper. Read up before agreeing on extra vaccinations and avoid unnecessary vaccinations or parasite treatments.

- It is necessary that they be neutered or spayed.

- Maintain a proper weight for your dog. You should be able to feel his ribs but they do not stick out. He or she will have their weight checked at the vet and this will inform you on your dogs optimal weight.

- Plenty of play-time outside with proper supervision.

- Daily long walks, play, sport, or games. "Limit time in front of the television."

~ Paws On – Paws Off ~

Handle Me Gently

Teaching your Bully to be still, calm, and patient while he is being handled is a very important step. When you master this one it will make life easier for both of you when either at the groomer or the vet. It also helps when there is unwanted or accidental touching and especially when dealing with small children who love to handle dogs in all sorts of unusual and not so regular ways. This one will take patience and a few tricks to get it started. Remember, it is important to begin handling your new puppy immediately after you find each other and are living together.

-It is important to understand that muzzles are not bad and do not hurt dogs. They can be an effective device and a great safety feature when your dog is learning to be handled. Easy cheese or peanut butter spread on the floor or on the refrigerator door should keep him in place while he learns to be handled. If he does not like to be handled, he can learn to accept it. You must practice this with your dog for at least one to three minutes each day so that he becomes comfortable with touch. All dogs are unique and therefore some will accept this easier and quicker than others will. This will be a life-long process.

With all of the following exercises, follow these steps:

- Begin with short, non-intrusive gentle touching. If he is calm and he is not trying to wiggle away, give him a treat.

- If he wiggles, keep touching him but do not fight his movements, keeping your hands on him lightly and while moving with him. When he settles, treat him and remove your hands.

- Work from one second to ten seconds where applicable, working your way up 2,4,6,8 to 10 seconds.

- Do not go on to another step until he adapts to, and enjoys the current one.

- *Do not* work these exercises more than a few minutes at a time. Overstimulation can cause your dog stress.

Handling the Dog's Body

The Collar

Find a quiet place to practice, get treats, and put your puppy's collar on.

- While gently restrained, touch him under his chin below his collar, and then release him right away simultaneously treating him. Do this about ten times or until your dog seems comfortable and happy with it.

- Grab and hold the collar where it is under his chin and hold it for about 2 seconds, treat, and repeat. Increase the amount of time until you have achieved about ten seconds of holding and your dog remains calm. Treat after each elapsed amount of time. Work your way up 2,4,6,8 to 10 seconds of holding.

- Hold the collar under his chin and now give it a little tug. If he accepts this and does not resist, treat, and repeat. If he wiggles, keep a gentle hold on the collar until he calms down, and then treat and release him. Repeat this step until he is happy with it. Now, switch to the top of the collar and repeat the whole progression again. Remember to increase the time held and the intensity of the tug using a slow pace. You can pull or tug, but do not jerk your dog's neck or head, as this could cause injury and interfere with your outcome objectives of the training exercise.

Paws in the clause

It is a fact that most dogs do not like to have their paws touched. Go slow with this exercise. The eventual goal is for your puppy to adore his paws being fondled. In the following exercises, any time he does not wiggle and try to get away, treat him up. If he does wiggle, stay with him using gentle contact, and then treat and release when he calms down. Each one of these steps will take a few days to complete and will require a dozen repetitions. Make sure you successfully complete each step and your puppy is at least tolerant of the contact before you go on to the next one. *-Do each step with all four paws, and remember to pause between paws.*

- Pick up his paw and immediately give him a treat. Repeat this five times and then progress adding an additional one second each time until ten seconds is reached.

- Hold the paw for ten-seconds.

- Hold the paw and move it around.

- Massage the paw.

- Pretend to trim the nails.

Side Note: Do not trim your dog's nails unless you are positively sure you know what you are doing. It is not easy and it can cause extreme pain to your dog if you are not properly trained.

Do you ear what I ear?

- Reach around the side of your dog's head, and then briefly and gently touch his ear. Treat and repeat ten times.

- When he is comfortable with this, practice holding the ear for one-second. If he is calm, treat. If he wiggles, stay with him until he is calm, then treat and release. Do this until ten seconds is completed with no wiggling.

- Manipulate his ear. Pretend to clean the ear. Do this gently and slowly so that your dog learns to enjoy it. It will take a few days of practice until your dog is calm enough for the real ear cleaning part. If your dog is already sensitive about his ears being touched, it will take longer.

From the mouth of dog's

- Gently touch your dog's mouth, treat, and repeat ten times.

- Touch the side of his mouth and lift a lip to expose a tooth. Treat and release only after he stops resisting.

- Gently and slowly, lift the lip to expose more and more teeth on both sides of the mouth, and then open the mouth. Treat and release when he does not resist. Be cautious with this one.

- Touch a tooth with a toothbrush, then work up to brushing his teeth for one to ten-seconds.

A tell of the tail

Many dogs are sensitive about having their tails handled, and rightly so. Think about if someone grabs you by the arm and you are not fully ready. That is similar to the reaction a dog feels when grabbed, especially when their tails are handled.

- Start by briefly touching his tail. When moving to touch your dog's tail move slowly and let your hand be seen moving towards his tail. This keeps your dog from being startled. Repeat this ten times with treats until you notice your dog is comfortable with his tail being touched.

- Increase the duration of time you hold his tail until you achieve the ten-second mark.

- Tenderly and cautiously, pull the tail up, brush the tail, then give the tail a gentle tug.

Children, 'nuff said

You must prepare your poor dog to deal with the strange, unwelcome touching that is often exacted on them by children. Alternatively, you could just put a sign around his neck that says; "You must be at least 18 to touch this dog." However, it is very likely that you will encounter children that are touchy, grabby, or pokey.

- Prepare your dog for the strange touches that children may perpetrate. Prepare him by practicing and treating him for accepting these odd bits of contact like ear tugs, tail tugs, and perhaps a little harder than usual head pats, kisses, and hugs. Keep in mind, as we said before, dogs and kids are not a natural pairing, but cheese and wine are. Even a dog that is *good with kids* can be pushed to a breaking point and then things can get ugly.

Always supervise children around your dog. ALWAYS! – it is a dog ownership law

Can you give me a lift?

An emergency may arise that requires you to pick up your dog. Again, move and proceed slowly and cautiously. First, you put your arms around him briefly and then give him a treat if he stays still. Increase the time duration with successive repetitions. Next, slowly proceed lifting him off the ground and back down, and treat when he does not wriggle. Increase the time and the distance you that you lift him from the ground. Eventually, you will be able to prepare him, with ease, for the groomer or the vet by lifting him up and placing him on a table. If you own an extra large dog, or dog that is too heavy for you to lift, solicit help for this training from family or a friend. Gigantor may take two to lift safely and properly.

Once up on the table you can practice handling in ways a groomer or veterinarian might handle your dog. This is good preparation for a day at the dog spa or veterinary procedures.

The brush off

- Get your puppy's brush and lightly touch him with it all over his body. If he remains unmoving, give him a treat and repeat. Repeat this until you can brush his whole body and he does not move.

Your puppy will become comfortable with all varieties of touching and handling if you work slowly, patiently and with plenty of good treats. It is a very important step in his socialization to make him comfortable with being handled.

~ *Paws On – Paws Off* ~

Giving Treats

Treats, treats, *treats!* *"Come and get 'em."* How many times have you heard a friend or family member tell you about some crazy food that their dog loves? Dogs do love a massive variety of foods; unfortunately, not all of the foods that they think they want to eat are good for them. Dog treating is not rocket science but it does take a little research, common sense, and paying attention to how your dog reacts after wolfing down a treat.

I am going to throw out some ideas for treats for training as well as some regular ole "Good Dog" treats for your sidekick and friend in mischief. I will touch on the proper time to treat, the act of giving the treat, types of treats, and bribery vs. reward.

Types of Treats

Love and attention is considered a reward and is certainly a positive reinforcement that can be just as effective as an edible treat. Dog treating is comprised of edibles, praise, love, and attention. Engaging in play or allowing some quality time with their favorite piece of rawhide is also effectual. At times, these treats are crucial to dog training.

Human foods that are safe for dogs, include most fruits and veggies, cut up meats that are raw or cooked, yogurt, peanut butter, kibble, and whatever else you discover that your dog likes, but be sure that it is good for him, in particular his digestive system. Remember, not all human foods are good for dogs. Please read up on the dos and don'ts regarding human foods and dogs. A "treat" is considered something about the size of a kernel of corn. All a dog needs is a little taste to keep him interested. The kernel size is something that is swiftly eaten and swallowed, making it non-distracting from training. Remember, a treat is just quick tasted, used for enticement and reinforcement.

Giving the Treat

Try to avoid treating your dog when he is over stimulated and running amuck in an unfocused state of mind. This can be counterproductive and might reinforce a negative behavior resulting in you not being able to get your dog's attention.

When giving the treat, allow your dog to get a big doggie whiff of that nibble of tasty food treat, but keep it up and away from a possible attempt at a quick snatch and grab. Due to their keen sense of smell, they will know long before you figure it out that there is a tasty snack nearby. Issue your command and wait for him to obey before presenting the doggie reward. Remember when dog treating, it is important to be patient and loving, but it is equally important not to give the treat until he obeys. Try to use treating to reward the kickback mellow dog, not the out of control or over-excited dog.

Some dogs have a natural gentleness to them and always take from your hand gently, while other dogs need some guidance to achieve this. If your dog is a bit rough during treat grabbing, go ahead and train the command "gentle!" when giving treats. Be firm from this point forward. Give up no treats unless taken gently. Being steadfast with your decision to implement this, and soon your pup or dog will comply, if he wants the tasty treat.

Time to Treat

The best time to be issuing dog treats is in between his or her meals. During training, always keep the tastiest treat in reserve in case you need to reel in your dog's attention back to the current training session. It is good to keep in mind that treating too close to meal times makes all treats less effective, so remember this when planning your training sessions. Obviously, if your dog is full from mealtime he will be less likely to want a treat reward than if he is a bit hungry, therefore your training session will likely be more difficult and far less effective.

What's In the Treats?

Before purchasing, look at the ingredients on the treat packaging, and make certain there are no chemicals, fillers, additives, colors and things that are unhealthy. Certain human foods that are tasty to us might not be so tasty to your dog, and he will tell you. Almost all dogs love some type of raw or cooked meats. In tiny nibble sizes (size of a corn kernel), these treats work great to get their attention where you want it focused.

Many people like to make homemade treats and that is fine, just keep to the rules we just mentioned and watch what you are adding while you are having fun in the kitchen. Remember to research and read the list of vegetables dogs can and cannot eat, and note that pits and seeds can cause choking and intestinal issues, such as dreaded doggy flatulence. Remove the seeds and pits, and clean all fruits and veggies before slicing it into doggie size treats.

Bribery vs. Reward Dog Treating

The other day a friend of mine mentioned *bribery* for an action when he wanted his dog to shake his hand. I thought about it later and thought I would clarify for my readers. *Bribery* is the act of offering the food in advance to get the dog to act out a command or behavior. *Reward* is giving your dog his favorite toy, food, love, affection *after* he has performed the behavior.

An example of bribery would be, if you want your dog to come and you hold out in front of you in your hand a huge slab of steak before calling him. Reward would be giving your dog the steak after he obeyed the "come!" command.

Bribed dogs learn to comply with your wishes only when they *see* food. The rewarded dog realizes that he only gets his reward after performing the desired action. This also assists by introducing non-food items as rewards when training and treating. Rewards such as play, toys, affection, and praise can be substituted for treats.

Dog Nutrition

As for nutrition, humans study it, practice it, complain about it, but usually give into the science of it. Like humans, dogs have their own nutrition charts to follow, and are subject to different theories and scientific studies, as well.

In the following, we will look at the history of dog food, as well as the common sense of raw foods, nutrient lists, and what your dog might have to bark about regarding what he is ingesting.

In the beginning, there were wild packs of canines everywhere and they ate anything that they could get their paws on. Similar to human survival, dogs depended upon meat from kills, grasses, berries, and other edibles that nature provided them. Guess what the great news is? Many millennia later nature is still providing all that we need.

Some History

In history, the Romans wrote about feeding their dogs barley bread soaked in milk along with the bones of sheep. The wealthy Europeans of the 1800's would feed their dogs better food than most humans had to eat. Meat from horses and other dead animals was often rounded up from the streets to recycle as dog food for the rich estates on the outskirts of the city. Royalty is legendary for pampering their dogs with all sorts of delicacies from around the world. Meanwhile, the poor and their dogs had to fend for themselves or starve. Being fed table scraps from a pauper's diet was not sufficient to keep a dog healthy, and the humans themselves often had their own nutrition problems. To keep from starving dogs would hunt rats, rabbits, mice, and any other rodent type creature they could sink their teeth.

Other references from the 18th century tell of how the French would mix breadcrumbs with tiny pieces of meat for their dogs. It is also written that the liver, heart, blood, or all, were mixed with milk or cheese and sometimes bread was a manmade food source for domestic canine. In England, they would offer soups flavored with meat and bone to augment their dog's nutrition.

In the mid to late 1800's a middle class blossomed out of the industrial revolution. This group started taking on dogs as house pets and unwittingly created an enterprise out of feeding household pets that were suddenly in abundance. This new class with its burgeoning wealth had extra money to spend. Noting that the sailor's biscuits kept well for long periods, James Spratt began selling his own recipe of hard biscuit for dogs in London, and shortly thereafter, he took his new product to New York City. It is believed that he single-handedly started the American dog food business. This places the dog food and kibble industry at just over 150 years old, and now is an annual multi-billion dollar business.

All the while we know that any farm dog, or for that matter, any dog that can kill something and eat it will do just that. Nothing has changed throughout the centuries.

Raw meat does not kill dogs, so it is safe to say that raw food diets will not either.

Raw Food Stuff

Let us take a look-see at the raw food diet for canines. First remember our dogs, pals, best friends, comedy actors, were meant to eat real food such as meat. Their DNA does not only dictate them to eat dry cereals that were concocted by humans in white lab coats. These cereals based and meat-by product may have been keeping our pets alive, but possibly not thriving at optimum levels.

There are many arguments for the benefits of real and raw foods. Sure it is more work, but isn't their health worth it? It is normal, not abnormal to be feeding your dog, a living food diet; it is thought that it will greatly boost their immune system and over-all health. *All foods,* dry, wet, or raw contain a risk, as they can all contain contaminants and parasites.

There are different types of raw food diets. There are raw meats that you can prepare at home by freeze-drying or freezing that you can easily thaw to feed your dog.

Raw food diets amount to foods that are not cooked or sent through a processing plant. With some research, you can make a decision on what you think is the best type of diet for your dog. For your dog's health and for their optimal benefits it is worth the efforts of your research time to read up on a raw foods diet or possibly a mix of kibble and raw foods.

Rules of thumb to follow for a raw food diet

1. Before switching, make sure your dog has a healthy gastro-intestinal track.

2. Be smart and do not leave meat un-refrigerated for lengthy periods.

3. To be safe, simply follow human protocol for food safety. Toss out the smelly, slimy, or the meat and other food items that just do not seem right.

4. Keep it balanced. Correct amount of vitamins and minerals, fiber, antioxidants, and fatty acids. Note any medical issues your dog has and possible diet correlations.

5. A gradual switch over between foods is recommended to allow their GI track to adjust. Use new foods as a treat, and then watch stools to see how the dog is adjusting.

6. Take note of the size and type of bones you throw to your dog. Not all dogs do well with real raw bones.

7. Freezing meats for three days, similar to sushi protocol, can help kill unwanted pathogens or parasites.

8. Take note about what is working and not working with your dog's food changes Remember to be vigilant, and take note of your observations when tracking a new diet.

9. Like us humans, most dogs do well with a variety of foods. There is no one-size-fits-all diet.

10. Please read up on raw foods diet before switching over, and follow all veterinary guidelines.

Human Foods for Dogs

Many human foods are safe for dogs. In reality, human and dog foods were similar for most of our coexistence. Well, maybe we wouldn't eat some of the vermin they eat, but if we were hungry enough we could. Whether you have your dog on a raw food diet, a partial raw food diet, or manufactured dog foods, you can still treat with some human foods. Even a top quality dog food may be lacking in some nutrients your dog may need. In addition, a tasty safe human food, such as an apple can be used as a treat in training. Below is a short list of some safe human foods that you may feed your dog. Remember to proceed in moderation to see how your dog's digestive system reacts and adjusts to each different food. Always keep plenty of clean fresh drinking water available for your dog.

Short List of SAFE Human Foods for Dogs

Oatmeal

Oatmeal is a fantastic alternative human food source for grain for dogs that are allergic to wheat. Oatmeal's fiber can also be beneficial to more mature dogs. A general set of rules can be followed when feeding your dog oatmeal. Limit the serving sizes, and amount of serving times per week, be sure to serve the oatmeal fully cooked, and finally never add any sugar or additional flavoring.

Apples

REMOVE the seeds. Apples are an excellent human food safe for dogs to crunch on. My dog loves to munch on apples. Apples offer small amounts of both vitamin C and Vitamin A. They are a good source of fiber for a dog of any age. Caution! Do not let your dog eat the seeds of the apple OR the core as they are known to contain minute amounts of cyanide. A few will not be detrimental, so do not freak out if it happens. Just be cautious and avoid the core and seeds when treating.

Brewers Yeast

After alcohol is made, what is left over is 'brewer's yeast.' This powder has a tangy taste that dogs will clamber over. The yeast is rich in B vitamins, which are great for the dog's skin, nails, ears, and coat. Do not confuse this with 'baking yeast,' which can make your dog ill if eaten. All you need to do is add a couple of sprinkles of brewer's yeast on your dog's food to spice it up. Most dogs really enjoy this stuff.

Eggs

Does your dog need a protein boost? Eggs are a super supplemental food because they contain ample amounts of protein, selenium, and riboflavin. They are also easily digested by your pooch. Cook your egg(s) before serving them to your best buddy, because the cooking process makes more protein available, and it make them more digestible. Eggs are good for energy, strength, and great for training as well.

Green Beans

A Lean dog is a happier, more energetic dog. Feeding your dog, cooked green beans is a good source of manganese, and vitamins C and K, and is considered a good source of fiber. If you have a lazier dog living 'A Dog's Life' then it is good to be proactive with your dog's weight. Add a steady stream of fresh green beans in your dog's diet for all the right reasons. Avoid salt.

Sweet Potatoes

Vitamin C, B-6, manganese, beta-carotene, and fiber can be found in sweet potatoes. Slice them up and dehydrate and you have just found a great new healthy source for treating your dog. Next time you are out shopping for potatoes, pick up sweet potatoes, and see if your best little buddy takes to them. My bet is that your dog will love them.

Pumpkins

A pumpkin is a fantastic source of vitamin A, fiber, and beta-carotene. Trend towards a healthy diet with plenty of fiber and all the essential vitamins and proteins your dog needs. Pumpkin is one way to help you mix it up a bit. Feed it dried or moist, separate as a treat, or with his favorite bowl. Feed it as a treat, dried or moist, or in his favorite bowl. Pumpkin can be a fantastic, fun, and natural alternative food for dogs.

Salmon

A great source of omega 3 fatty acids, salmon is an excellent food that can support your dog's immune system, as well as his skin, coat, and overall health. Some dog owners notice when adding salmon to their dog's diet that it increases resistance to allergies. Be sure to cook the salmon before serving it. You can use salmon oil too. For treats, added flavoring to a meal, or as a complete meal, salmon is a fantastic source of natural, real food that is safe for dogs..

Flax Seed

Grounded or in oil form, flax seed is a nourishing source of omega 3 fatty acids. Omega 3 fatty acids are essential in helping your dog maintain good skin and a shiny healthy coat. Note; you will want to serve the flax seed directly after grinding it because this type of fatty acid can turn sour soon after. Flax seed is also a wonderful source of fiber your dog or puppy needs.

Yogurt

Always a great source for your dog's calcium and protein, yogurt is another one of our top ten human foods safe for dogs. Pick a fat free yogurt with no added sweeteners, or artificial sugar, color or flavoring.

Melons

Also, great for your dog is watermelons, cantaloupes, honeydews. Without prior research, avoid any exotic melons or fruits.

Peanut butter

Yep, a big spoon full and it will keep him occupied for a while.

Berries (fresh & frozen)

Blueberries, blackberries, strawberries, huckleberries or raspberries provide an easy and tasty snack.

Cooked chicken

Chicken sliced up is a favorite yummy snack for your K9 to enjoy in addition, or in place of his regular meal.

Cheese

Sliced or cubed pieces are great for training or in the place of food. A tablespoon of cottage cheese on top of your dog's food will certainly be a healthy hit. Try using easy to use string cheese as a training teat.

Bananas

All fruits have phytonutrients, and other required nutrients that are essential to your canine's health.

Carrots

Crunchy veggies are good for the teeth. Carrots are full of fiber and vitamin A.

UNSAFE Human Foods

Below is a list of harmful foods for dogs. This is not a complete list, but a common list of foods known to be harmful to our k9 friends. If you are unsure of a food that you wish to add to your dog's diet, please consult a veterinarian or expert on dog nutrition.

Onions: Both onions and garlic contain the toxic ingredient thiosulphate. However, onions are more dangerous than garlic because of this toxin. Many dog biscuits contain *trace* amounts of garlic, and because of this small amount, there is no threat to the health of your dog. This poison can be toxic in one large dose, or with repeated consumption that builds to the toxic level in the dog's blood.

Chocolate: Contains theobromine, a compound that is a cardiac stimulant and a diuretic. This can be fatal to dogs.

Grapes: Contains an unknown toxin that can affect kidney, and in large enough amounts can cause acute kidney failure.

Raisins: (Same as above)

Most Fruit Pits and Seeds: Contains cyanogenic glycosides, which if consumed can cause cyanide poisoning. The fruits by themselves are okay to consume.

Macadamia Nuts: Contains an unknown toxin that can be fatal to dogs.

Most Bones: Should not be given (especially chicken bones) because they can splinter and cause a laceration of the digestive system or pose a choking hazard because of the possibility for them to become lodged in your pet's throat.

Potato Peelings and Green Potatoes: Contains oxalates, which can affect the digestive, nervous, and urinary systems.

Rhubarb leaves: Contains high amount of oxalates.

Broccoli: Broccoli should be avoided, though it is only dangerous in large amounts.

Green parts of tomatoes: Contains oxalates, which can affect the digestive, nervous, and urinary systems.

Yeast dough: Can produce gas and swell in your pet's stomach and intestines, possibly leading to a rupture of the digestive system.

Coffee and tea: (due to the caffeine)

Alcoholic Beverages: Alcohol is very toxic to dogs and can lead to coma or even death.

Human Vitamins: Vitamins containing iron are especially dangerous. These vitamins can cause damage to the lining of the digestive system, the kidneys, and liver.

Moldy or spoiled foods: There are many possible harmful outcomes from spoiled foods.

Persimmons: These can cause intestinal blockage.

Raw Eggs: Salmonella.

Salt: In large doses can cause an electrolyte imbalance.

Mushrooms: Can cause liver and kidney damage.

Avocados: Avocado leaves; fruit, seeds, and bark contain a toxin known as persin. The Guatemalan variety that is commonly found in stores appears to be the most problematic. Avocados are known to cause respiratory distress in other animals, but causes less harmful problems in dogs. It is best to avoid feeding them to your dog.

Xylitol: This artificial sweetener is not healthy for dogs.

~ *Paws On – Paws Off* ~

According to nutritional scientists and veterinarian health professionals, your dog needs twenty Amino Acids, and ten of which are essential. At least thirty-six nutrients and a couple of extra may be needed to combat certain afflictions. Your dog's health depends upon the intake of the following nutrients. Read labels and literature to take stock of the foods you provide.

36 Nutrients for dogs:

1. 10 essential Amino Acids – Arginine, Histidine, Isoleucine, Leucine, Lysine, Methionine. Along with Phenylalanine, Threonine, Tryptophan, and Valine.

2. 11 vitamins – A, D, E, B1, B3, B5, B6, B12, Folic Acid, and Choline.

3. 12 minerals – Calcium, Phosphorus, Potassium, Sodium, Chloride, Magnesium, Copper, Manganese, Zinc, Iodine, and Selenium

4. Fat – Linoleic Acid

5.Omega 6 Fatty Acid

6.Protein

Suggested Daily Quantities of Recommended Nutrients		
Nutrient	Puppies	Adult Dogs
Protein (%)	22.0	18.0
Arginine (%)	0.62	0.51
Histidine (%)	0.22	0.18
Isoleucine (%)	0.45	0.37
Leucine (%)	0.72	0.59
Lysine (%)	0.77	0.63
Methionine + cystine (%)	0.53	0.43
Phenylalanine + tyrosine (%)	0.89	0.73
Threonine (%)	0.58	0.48
Tryptophan (%)	0.20	0.16
Valine (%)	0.48	0.39
Fat (%)	8.0	5.0
Calcium (%)	1.0	0.6
Phosphorus (%)	0.8	0.5
Sodium (%)	0.3	0.06
Chloride (%)	0.45	0.06

We realize it may take time to understand what kind of diet your dog will thrive. Do your best to include in your dogs daily diet, all thirty-six nutrients mentioned here. All of which can come from fruits, veggies, kibble, raw foods, and yes, even good table scraps. You will soon discover that your dog has preferred foods. For your dog to maintain optimum health, he needs a daily basis of a GI track healthy, well-rounded diet with a good balance of exercise, rest, socializing, care, and love.

~ Paws On – Paws Off ~

Dog Socialization

What, Where, When, Why

Everyone reads or hears socialization mentioned when reading about dogs and puppies. What is the reason for socialization? When is the best time to socialize my shiny new puppy? These and more are questions you often hear asked. Does it has to do with getting along well with other dogs and people or is there more to it? Do I let them loose with other dogs and puppies, and just sit back, and watch? Let us begin by looking at how a puppy's social development process is played out from puppy to adulthood.

Socialization is learning and maintaining acceptable behavior in any situation, especially when your dog or puppy does not want too. The goal is learning to handle any normal experience that occurs in life without becoming overly stimulated, fearful, reactive, or aggressive.

Socialization summary

- Learning to remain calm when the world is buzzing around them.

- Exposure in a safe manner to the environment that will encompass his or her world, including the rules and guidelines that accompany it.

- Learning to respond to signals when they do not want too. For example, In the midst of a tail chasing session with a fellow puppy or the irresistible squirrel.

The first phase of socialization begins as early as 3 weeks and lasts to approximately 12 weeks old, during this time puppies discover that they are dogs and begin to play with their littermates. Survival techniques that they will use throughout their lives, such as biting, barking, chasing, and fighting, begin to be acted out. Concurrently during this time-period, puppies experience big changes socially and physically. Learning submissive postures and taking corrections from their mother, interaction with their littermates begin to teach them about hierarchies. Keeping mother and puppies together for at least 7 weeks tends to increase their ability to get along well with other dogs and learn more about themselves and their actions, such as the force of a bite on their brothers and sisters.

Between the ages of 7-12 weeks, a period of rapid learning occurs and they learn what humans are, and whether to accept them as safe. This is a crucial period, and has the *greatest impact* on *all future social behavior*. This is the time we begin teaching puppies the acceptable rules of conduct. Take note that they have a short attention span, and physical limitations. This is the easiest period to get your puppy comfortable with new things, and the chance to thwart later behavioral issues that stem from improper or incomplete socialization. Puppies are not out of harm's way from all diseases at this time, but the risk is relatively low because of primary vaccines, good care, and mother's milk immunity. Behavioral problems are the greatest threat to the owner-dog bond and the number one cause of death to dogs under 3 years of age.

Enrolling your puppy in classes before 3 months of age is an outstanding avenue to improving socialization, training, and strengthening the bond between you and your puppy. You can begin socialization classes as early as 7-8 weeks. The recommendation is to have your puppy receive at least 1 set of vaccines, and a de-worming 7 days prior to starting the first class.

From birth, puppies should be exposed to handling and manipulation of body parts, and exposure to different people, places, situations, well socialized animals, and more. Encourage your puppies exploring, curiosity, and investigation of different environments. Games, toys, and a variety of surfaces such as steps, tile, concrete, tunnels, are all things to expose your puppy too and should continue into adulthood to keep your dog sociable and not shy.

It is important for your puppy to be comfortable playing, sleeping, or exploring alone. Schedule alone play with toys, and solo naps in their crate or another safe area. This teaches them to entertain themselves and not become overly attached, or have separation issues with their owners. Getting them comfortable with their crate is also beneficial for travel and to use as a safe area for your puppy to relax and feel safe.

Having knowledge of your breed and puppy will help in understanding their social predispositions. Some breeds that act as sporting and companion dogs will carry puppy sociability into adulthood. Terriers, guard, herding, and bully dogs become less tolerant while others consistently challenge or remain passive. Which is your breed's disposition?

Two phases of fear imprinting occur in your growing puppy's life. *A fear period is a stage during which your puppy or dog may be more apt to perceive certain stimuli as threatening.* During these two periods, any event your puppy thinks is traumatic can leave a lasting effect, possibly forever. The first period is from 8-11 weeks and the second is between 6-14months of age. During this period, you will want to keep your puppy clear of any frightening situations, but that is not always easy to determine. A chrome balloon on the floor could possibly scare the "bejeebers" out of your little pup. There is no one size fits all here in knowing what is fearful for your puppy. Becoming familiar with canine body language can help you diagnose your pups fear factor. The second period often reflects the dog becoming more reactive or apprehensive about new things. Larger breeds sometimes have an extended second period.

Keep a few things in mind when seeking play dates for socialization of your puppy. A stellar puppy class will have a safe, mature dog for the puppies to learn boundaries and other behaviors. When making play dates, puppies should be matched by personality and play styles. Games, such as retrieve or drop, help to curb possessive behaviors, as well as to help them learn to give up unsafe or off limits items, so they can be taken them out of harm's way. Another important lesson during play is for puppies to learn to come back to their human. *Your dog should be willingly dependent upon you and look to you for guidance.*

Teach mature easily stimulated dogs to relax before they are permitted to socialize with others. If you have an adult dog that enjoys flying solo, do not force them into situations. Teach your dogs and puppies less aroused play and encourage passive play. This includes play that does not encompass dominance, mouthing, or biting other puppies. If you have rough play happening between multiple dogs or puppies, then interrupt the rough housing by frequently calling them to you and rewarding their attention. The attention then is turned to you. As a distraction to dissuade mouthing contact, try to interject toys into the play. Elevated play can lead to aggression as they grow, especially breeds that can easily get to full arousal in seconds.

Proper socialization requires patience, kindness, and consistency while teaching. You and your dog should both be having fun during this process. If you think, your dog may have a socialization issue seek professional advice from a qualified behavioral person.

~ Paws On – Paws Off ~

Why Clicker Training?

The important reason I put this information together is that it is essential to understand why timing and consistency is important, and why clicker training works. If any of this is confusing, do not worry, because I walk you through the training process, step-by-step.

Clicker training started over seventy years ago and has become a tried and true method for training dogs and other animals. The outcome of using a clicker is an example of conditioned reinforcement. Rewarding the animal in combination with clicker use has proven highly effective as a positive reinforcement training method. It is a humane and effective way of training dogs without instilling fear for non-compliance. I know that my mother wished she would have known about clicker training when my brother and I were growing up. I am sure she would have put the clicker into action so my brother would place his dirty clothes inside the bin, rather than on the floor.

In the 1950s, Keller Breland, a pioneer in animal training, used a clicker while training many different species of animals, including marine mammals. He met great success using this method of training on these animals. His system developed for clicker training marine mammals is still in use today. Keller also trained dogs using the clicker. Because of its effectiveness, it was brought into use by others in the dog training community. Gradually, clicker training for dogs gained more and more popularity and by the early 1980's its use became widespread. The success of the clicker spans 7 decades and now is a widely accepted standard for dog training.

A trainer will use the clicker to mark desired actions as they occur. At the exact instant, the animal performs the desired action, the trainer clicks and promptly delivers a food reward or other reinforcements. One key to clicker training is the trainer's timing, as *timing is crucial*. For example, clicking and rewarding slightly too early or too late will reinforce the action that is occurring at that very instant rather than the action you were targeting the reward for. The saying goes, "you get what you click for."

Clicker trainers often use the process of *shaping*. Shaping is the process of gradual transformation of a specific action into the desired action by rewarding each successive progression towards the desired action. This is done by gradually molding or training the dog to perform a specific response by first, reinforcing the small, successive responses that are similar to the desired response, instead of waiting for the perfect completion to occur. The trainer looks for small progressions that are heading in the direction towards the total completion of the desired action and then clicks and treats. It is important to recognize and reward those tiny steps made in the target direction. During training, the objective is to create opportunities for your dog to earn frequent rewards. In the beginning, it is acceptable to increase the frequency of C/T to every 3-4 seconds, or less. By gauging the dog's abilities and improvements, the trainer can gradually increase the length of time between C/T. It is necessary to assess the dog's progress from moment to moment, adjusting C/T to achieve the desired actionable outcome.

During training, and in conjunction with clicker use, the introduction of a cue word or hand signal can be applied. Eventually, the clicker can be phased out in favor of a cue or cues that have been reinforced during the training sessions. As a result, your dog will immediately respond by reacting, obeying, and performing actions to your hand gestures or verbal commands. Watching this unfold is a highly satisfying process, which empowers your friend to be the best he can, and while you have fulfilled your role as *alpha* and pack leader.

Why is clicking effective over using a word cue first?

The clicking sound is a unique sound that is not found in nature, and it is more precise than a verbal command. Verbal commands can be confusing because the human voice has many tonal variations, where as the clicker consistently makes a sound that your dog will not confuse with any other noise. It is also effective because it is directed at him and followed by good things. Therefore, your dog completely understands which action is desired and your dog will quickly understand that the click is followed by a reward.

The clicker sound is produced in a quick and accurate way that is in response to the slightest actions that your dog makes. This clarity of function of this tool increases the bond between you and your dog, as a result making your dog more interested in the training sessions, and ultimately your relationship more engaging and entertaining. Dare I say fun? On that note, do not forget to always have fun and add variety to your training sessions. Variety is the spice of life, mix up those treats, rewards, and commands.

Clicker training works this way

At the *exact* instant the action occurs, the trainer clicks. If a dog begins to *sit*, the trainer recognizes that, and at the exact moment the dog's buttocks hits the ground the trainer clicks and offers the dog a reward. Usually the reward is a small kernel sized food treat, but a reward can be a toy, play, or affection. Whatever the dog enjoys is a reward worth giving.

In as soon as 2-3 clicks have been issued a dog will associate the sound of the click with something it enjoys. Once the association is made, it will repeat the action it did when hearing the click. Click = Reward. When this goes off in the dog's head, repeating the action makes sense.

The three steps are as follows:

1. *Get the action* you request

2. *Mark the action* with your clicker

3. *Reinforce the action* with a reward

How do you ask for actions when clicker training your dog?

During clicker training before adding a cue command such as "stay," you wait until your dog completely understands the action. A cue is the name of the action or it can be a hand signal that you are using when you ask your dog to perform a specific action. Your dog should know the action *stay* from the click and reward before you verbally name it. He or she has connected being still to receiving a click and reward.

When training you do not want to add the 'cue' until your dog has been clicked 5-10 times for the action, and is accurately responding in a manner that clearly shows he understands which action earns the click and reward. This is called introducing the cue.

Teaching your dog the name of the cue or action requires saying or signaling before your dog repeats the action. After several repetitions, begin to click and reward when your dog performs the action, be sure the cue is given before the reward. Your dog will learn to listen and watch for the cue, knowing that if he does the action a reward will follow.

Clicker Training Help

If your dog is not obeying the cue, answer the following questions and then revise your training process so that your dog knows the meaning of the clicker sound cue during all situations. Importantly, be sure that your dog is and feels rewarded for doing the correct action.

Trainers never assume the dog is intentionally disobeying without asking the questions below.

1. Does your dog understand the meaning of the cue?

2. Does your dog understand the meaning of the cue in the situation first taught, but *not* in different situations that you gave the cue?

3. Is the *reward* for doing the action you want, satisfying your dog's needs? Is the treat or toy worth the effort?

Once you have answered these questions, change your training process to be certain that your dog understands the clicker/cue in all situations, including high distraction situations such as at a busy park. Then be sure your dog is adequately rewarded and that it is clear your dog feels it has been properly rewarded. This will help put you two back on the path of mutual understanding during your training sessions.

~ *Paws On – Paws Off* ~

That's All Folks

Believe me, this is not everything to know about dogs. Training your Bull Terrier is a lifelong endeavor. There are a myriad of other methods, tricks, tools, and things to teach and learn with him. You are never finished, but this is half of the fun of having a dog, as he or she is a constant work in progress. Your dog is living art.

Remember, it is important to think like your dog. Patience with your dog, as well as with yourself is vital. If you do this right, you will have a relationship and a bond that will last for years. The companionship of a dog can bring joy and friendship like none other. Keep this book handy and reference it often. In addition, look for other resources, such as training books or utilize experienced friends with dogs and have them share their successes and failures. Never stop broadening your training skills. Your efforts will serve to keep you and your Bull Terrier happy and healthy for a long, long time.

Thanks for reading! I hope you enjoyed this as much as I have enjoyed writing it. If this book helps you in your training please comment on Amazon.

~ Paws On – Paws Off ~

DON'T THiNK – BE, ALPHA DOG

I wrote this book to inform and instruct dog owners of the fundamentals for establishing and maintaining the *alpha* position within the household hierarchy. Inside the book you will learn how to live, lead, train, and love your dog in a ***non-physical 'alpha dog' way***. Leading from the *alpha*

position makes everything dog related *easier*. All dogs need to know where they are positioned within the family (pack), and to understand, and trust that their *alpha* will provide food, shelter, guidance, and affection towards them. Then life becomes *easier* for you and your dog.

Whether or not you have read one of my "Think Like a dog..." breed specific training books, I'm confident that this guide will assist you while you train your dog companion. With these 'alpha' fundamentals, your dog will obey your commands in critical situations, and follow your lead into a safer and happier life. Remember, having an obedient dog keeps other animals and humans safe.

A dog that respects his 'alpha' leader is easier to control, teach, and trust. He is more likely to obey your commands and respect your rules. Be the 'alpha' now.

~ Paps

"**Alpha Dog Secrets**" by Paul Allen Pearce

LEARN MORE:
http://www.amazon.com/dp/B00ICGQO40

Hey...Did I miss something?

STUMPED?

Got a Question about Your Bull Terrier?

Ask an Expert Now!

Facebook ~

https://www.facebook.com/newdogtimes

NewDogTimes ~

http://newdogtimes.com/

*It's where the **Bull Terrier Secrets** have been hidden - since their Ancestral Wolf Packs were forced to collide with Man...*

Wait Until You Learn This

About the Author

Paul Allen Pearce is the author of many breed specific "Think Like a Dog" & "Think Like Me" dog-training books, "Alpha Dog Secrets Revealed," and others. When his family duties allow, he spends his spare time outdoors with his two dogs Buck and Samson. He lives in the South Eastern part of the United States.

Think Like a Dog - but Don't Eat Your Poop!

<u>Visit us today!</u>

Share Our Links – Like us, Pin us, Feed it, Tweet it

and Twerk it – We Need Help Too!

Facebook ~

https://www.facebook.com/newdogtimes

NewDogTimes ~

http://newdogtimes.com

"Thanks for reading. I hope you enjoyed this as much as I have enjoyed writing it and training my dog!"

"Keep on training and loving your Now Zen Like 'Kung-Fu' dog. Please be patient, loving, and have fun while training your dog."

~ Paul Allen Pearce

LEARN MORE:

http://www.amazon.com/dp/B00ICGQO40

Bull Terrier Facts

Country of Origin: England

Other Names: English Bull Terrier, Standard Bull Terrier, Mini Bull Terrier, English Standard Bull Terrier, English Miniature Bull Terrier

Nicknames: Bully, Gladiator

Group: Terrier, Terriers

Purpose: Family dog

Size: Medium

Height: Standard Bull Terrier

Height: 20 - 24 inches (51 - 61 cm) Weight: 45 - 80 pounds (20 - 36 kg)

Miniature Bull Terrier

Height: 10 - 14 inches (25 - 33 cm) Weight: up to 24 - 33 pounds (11 - 15 kg)

Lifespan: 9-12 years

Litter Sizes: As many as 13

Colors: The primary colors consist of brindle, red and tri-color (black, white & tan and black, tan & white) with various shades between these.

Coat: Short, dens, and smooth

Shedding: Average

Apartment: Yes, active indoors, small back yard recommended.

Temperament: Loving, fun, fearless, loyal, and protective.

Exercise: Daily extensive cardio type exercise that includes long walks.

Training: They can be stubborn, heel, and basics such as no, stay, leave it, and need to be trained before reaching adulthood. Proper and thorough socialization and structure is a NECESSITY.

Notes: They are indoor dogs that do get cold easily, and are active indoors. Be watchful of possessiveness.

Bull Terrier Rescue

Bull Terriers are often acquired without any clear understanding of what goes into owning one, and these dogs often end up in the care of rescue groups, and are in need of adoption or fostering. If you are interested in adopting a Bully, a rescue group is a good place to start. I have listed a few below.

http://www.bullterrierrescue.org/available.html

http://bullterrierclubofamericarescue.com/cms_rescue/

Other Books

"Don't Think BE Alpha Dog Secrets Revealed"

"Think Like a Dog...but don't eat your poop!"
(Breed specific dog training series)

"Think Like Me...but don't eat your poop!
(Breed specific dog training series)

Contributing Editors | Content Attributions

Photos: Thanks to the photographers for sharing your photographs via Creative Commons.

Flickr:
SIT https://www.flickr.com/photos/hel62/3007684860
DOWN
https://www.flickr.com/photos/hel62/3007684674/in/photostream/
COME https://www.flickr.com/photos/rtadlock/5593734183
LEASH
https://www.flickr.com/photos/karljonsson/3665670861/in/photostream/
NAME https://www.flickr.com/photos/manicomi/7526264538
GO
https://www.flickr.com/photos/manicomi/7529463230/in/photostream/
JUMP https://www.flickr.com/photos/manicomi/11250800576
HOUSETRAIN
https://www.flickr.com/photos/vivatier/5555082399
LEAVE IT
https://www.flickr.com/photos/manicomi/8647278665/in/photostream/
DROP IT https://www.flickr.com/photos/rtadlock/3131972511
NUTRITION https://www.flickr.com/photos/thiane/4104206362
DIGGING https://www.flickr.com/photos/rtadlock/3206947433
RUNNING WITH STICK
https://www.flickr.com/photos/manicomi/8830302052
COVER RED
https://www.flickr.com/photos/thetxm/2124488619
COVER BUSHES
https://www.flickr.com/photos/greo77/3133809859
LOOKING UP
https://www.flickr.com/photos/rtadlock/5612059498/in/photostream/

Legal Disclaimer:

The author of **Paws On ~ Paws Off "Think Like a Dog...but don't eat your poop!,** Paul Allen Pearce is in no way responsible at any time for the action of your pet, not now or in the future. Animals, without warning, may cause injury to humans and/or other animals. Paul Allen Pearce is not responsible for attacks, bites, mauling', nor any other viciousness or any and all other damages. We strongly recommend that you exercise caution for the safety of self, the animal, and all around the animals while working with your dog. We are not liable for any animal or human medical conditions or results obtained from training. While all attempts have been made to verify information provided in this publication, neither the author nor the publisher assume any responsibility for errors, omissions or contrary interpretation of the subject matter contained herein. The publisher and author assume no responsibility or liability whatsoever on the behalf of any purchaser or reader of the material provided.

Made in the USA
San Bernardino, CA
19 March 2017